Dinghy and Board Sailing
WEATHER

Alan Watts

NAUTICAL BOOKS
MACMILLAN

By the same Author

Wind and Sailing Boats
Instant Weather Forecasting
Weather Forecasting Ashore and Afloat
Instant Wind Forecasting
Wind Pilot (five volumes)
Basic Windcraft
Cruising Weather

Line drawings by Peter Milne

Copyright © Alan Watts 1984

ISBN 0 333 34558 4

First published in Great Britain 1984 by
NAUTICAL BOOKS
An imprint of Macmillan London Limited
4 Little Essex Street
London WC2R 3LF

Associated companies throughout the world

Typeset by Wyvern Typesetting Ltd
Printed in Hong Kong

Contents

Preface

There are dinghies and boards and there is meteorology – and sometimes one wonders what they have in common. You pick up a met. text and it bristles with weather charts and diagrams which would make you a good professional weather forecaster, but do not do much to improve your performance round the buoys.

I have sat on both sides of this fence. I was at one time a professional forecaster and for most of my life I have sailed dinghies and when I stopped being the former I began to think deeply about how much of my formal met. training was really useful to me as a helmsman. I decided that not much of it was, and I had to do some research of my own and read up what people had written about the wind in the past before I found useful facts that were really helpful in winning races.

The results of that initial re-think on met. I first set down in a book published in 1965 called *Wind and Sailing Boats*. It sold quite well both here and in the USA, but it is now out of print and the time has come to up-date that book, adding ideas that have come to me since then and throwing out some of the less useful material.

However, this is not *Wind and Sailing Boats* re-written – it is quite a new book and couched in different terms altogether. In it are the results of a further seventeen years of giving lectures and writing books and articles on the subject of those bits of met. which intimately affect the small-craft sailor and how they can be used. Nonetheless, many of my ideas on the small-scale antics of the wind have not changed over the years and so the reader who may have seen the earlier book will find diagrams and explanations that are very like ones in the latter.

There is still a great reservoir of knowledge of the way the wind acts waiting to be tapped. You will find in Chapter 18 two examples of what help you can get once you settle down and study the ways of the wind. Luckily Richard Creagh-Osborne, who before his untimely death gave me the material, had had to study the way the seabreeze worked very deeply, because he was editing my *Wind Pilot* which his company published. The *Wind Pilot* went into the details of seabreeze behaviour in greater detail than I have been able to do here, but all the important facts are to be found again within these covers. So he was really in no more favoured position than anyone else who studies the way the seabreeze acts – he had just done his homework very thoroughly. That is something that anyone can do and it certainly pays off. Not every time – but every so often you become aware of conditions that you recognise will produce a certain wind shift or set of shifts and you are then ready to play them when they come.

The phenomenal rise of the sailboard means that a vastly greater number of potential users of the wind are now afloat in all kinds of venues, both mundane and exotic. If the dinghy is a device that demands intuition to sail it then the board needs a measure of clairvoyance unparalleled in the annals of yacht racing. With a dinghy at least there is a second or so between the arrival of a wind change on the foresail and its arrival at the helmsman. With a board there is nothing to tell what the micro-shift will be. Anything which gives the board sailor a greater grasp of the structure of the wind must be a help and the chapters on micro-wind near the end of the book could assist here in the ever-present struggle to react quicker and more positively to the small-scale shifts that a board sailor has to meet.

Whatever you sail, a deeper knowledge of the wind and how it shifts under certain conditions cannot be anything but help you sail more efficiently and it is to this end that *Dinghy and Board Sailing is* directed. I have covered as well as I can those things which may happen to the wind wherever you sail – on the coast; inland; up in some high valley or other between craggy mountains and also in the other hemisphere. Not everything has been covered, but my experience in talking to sailing audiences over a good number of years leads me to believe that you cannot help but find something of use to you in these pages. I hope you do and good luck – with the weather, you often need it.

I would like to thank librarians at the National Meteorological Library at Bracknell, Berks, who in the past found me so many useful publications and also librarians at the Colchester Institute who did the same. I would like to thank Howard Ogden of Ocean Windsurfing, Brightlingsea, Essex, who helped compile the Beaufort scale for boards. Also Sir Peter Johnson, a yachting writer in his own right, who has piloted this book into print.

Alan Watts
November 1982

1 Beginning on the Weather

Many books on sailing tell you to study the weather. This is because of the safety aspect and also because the only motive power of small sailing boats is the wind. However, very few actually then go on to tell you what to do about it. They take it for granted that you will pick up those aspects of weather knowledge that are of prime importance to you. So to this end you consult weather books and are often confronted with a great deal of what seems very deep met.

I believe that this prevents a goodly number of sailing people from getting to grips with the real things that matter to them. We who sail dinghies and boards need to know about one element above all others – the wind. Compared to that, knowledge of other even quite nasty things that happen, like cold deluges of rain or unseasonal snow showers, pales into insignificance.

The traditional hazards of the seagoer, namely fog and fire, are not things which much concern the dinghy sailor. All he wants to know is whether there will be too much wind or too little and after that, what its direction will be.

If you are a beginner, the wind which for the experienced is the best working breeze, namely Force 4 (11–16 knots) is probably too much for you, but if you stay in the shelter of creeks or river banks then Force 4 may only be Force 3 – a gentle breeze of between 7 and 10 knots. Should it be early morning or evening then what was or will be Force 4 during the afternoon will perhaps be only Force 2 – a light breeze of between 4 and 6 knots.

This is a favourite time for the new board sailors to practise the gentle art of balancing themselves at the same time as they learn to handle the wishbone because an evening or early morning wind will also be very much steadier than an afternoon one, or one that is building up in strength when the morning sun is rising higher in the sky. Not that we need restrict this to board sailors. Dinghy sailors, especially young children, will find learning the ropes easier when the wind is light and is not full of tricky shifts, but as soon as they progress just a little the unreliable evening wind, which is so often full of 'holes', will become too tame.

The wind direction with respect to the shoreline is also an important aspect when you are first learning to sail. The beginner should not start sailing off a beach or other shoreline when the wind is blowing from it out to sea. This is particularly the case with board sailing, because unless you are such a natural at the game that you never fall off – and how many are there of those? – you stand the risk of being blown out to sea or onto a further shore from which you will have to be rescued by someone. Luckily there are very few fatalities bred this way, but it is a sure means of getting a name for being a nuisance.

Having said which, launching a board into waves that are being built by an on-shore wind is also a tricky business as the light board is always being thrown up and back at you by the waves as they run in. So once again sailing off the beach is, for the newcomer, a light wind affair, but get into a lagoon or a creek and you can have more freedom. Sailing a dinghy off a shore under the same conditions makes for a damp start, but is easier than with a board especially as most dinghies will have a crew, one of whose duties is to get saturated in the breaking waves holding the boat head-to-wind as the dry-as-a-bone helmsman sorts the sheets out and gets the rudder settled on its gudgeons.

Sometimes before people have understood the importance of the side-area of a centreplate or dagger-board, the lee shore is where they will be found unable to tack out from the ever-present edge because in the shallows they cannot put the plate down sufficiently fast to stop the boat drifting sideways back onto the mud. This should not be the same hazard for the board sailor who must learn to manipulate his dagger-board with his feet before he can get anywhere.

Thus the wind speed and direction are perhaps the most important things to note when you are going out to learn to sail. With all the safety devices available today you will probably not drown if you come unstuck, but it is a nasty fright when you are capsized in a fast ebbing tideway and 'home' is receding at a rapid rate. However, having said all this most people learn to sail without taking any course in meteorology. So, you may ask, is there any point in wasting time learning about it – especially as it seems so complicated and worse, unsure?

Well, certainly when you start to sail the only important things you are concerned with are not going out in conditions that are too strong for you and with being circumspect about the wind direction and the tide. Yet you soon get beyond that stage and then you want to race and prove how good you are at handling your boat or board. Now things are different. With everyone else trying to steal a march on you – and often doing so – you want to be able to meet the windshifts more efficiently than the others as this way you win races. Here is where you have to have a certain met. knowledge because only when you recognise in the sky the signs of coming change can you hope to be ready for the shift when it arrives and then to make the right tactical decisions.

This understanding will only come slowly and you need to hang the knowledge on the skeleton of the forecasts. The forecasters, whatever snide remarks you may make about them, know more about what tomorrow's weather will be than you do. What the forecasters do not know, and cannot tell you, is what the next few minutes' weather will be. That is up to you and it is the person who makes a useful marriage between the forecasts and his own local observations who has most to gain from a knowledge of weather process.

For instance, the forecast may indicate that a cold front will cross the area where you are due to race later, but it will not tell you when. You have to know the cloud structure of cold fronts and where the wind shifts are to be found under them in order to use the warning from the Met. Office to good advantage at the time. Only when you see the dark line of heavy clouds bearing down on you, perhaps see the further shore obliterated by rain and note the tell-tale wisps of fractured stratus cloud hanging below the coming cloud-base are you in a position to say 'Here comes a veer of wind and I must warn the crew to be ready for a hefty squall. Sometime soon I should get on to starboard tack in order to meet this imminent shift, but can I do it without jeopardizing my chances of making the next mark?'. This is where knowledge of the 'models' of meteorology come into their own. The more you know about weather systems and can come to recognise which part of a depression or anticyclone you are in, the more able you will become at making sense of the shifts these systems bring and to guess what the wind will do next.

I have tried to make this book practical – because as a dinghy sailor first, and a weatherman second, I have the problems very much in mind. Only those bits of met. which are going to help dinghy and board sailors recognise and use windshifts are important. That, and such capsizing things as thunderstorms and other weather features that breed excessive gusts and squalls; the effects of shelter and how to assess the difference between wind strength in the lee and in the open. These and other aspects of weather as they affect the sailing winds are the important features that people sailing small boats will want to know about.

So we start with the forecasts and then go on to refine and develop what clues they may give you about the day's wind events. Those will very often come via weather changes and clouds will usually be the means by which they will reveal their presence. However, on cloudless days no such help is at hand and then you have to find other possible clues as to what is likely to happen to the wind and when. The sailing wind will be dictated by what the wind is about a couple of thousand feet up and this so-called 'gradient' wind is the one you recognise from the direction of the isobars on the TV weather maps. If you really want to understand the way the wind's micro-changes come about you have to latch on to the gradient wind and appreciate why the surface wind is different.

Wind shifts that take many hours to complete will usually be due to the way the pressure pattern changes in your vicinity and that means you have to recognise the way pressure systems like depressions are formed, grow and die away. Intimately mixed up with depressions are fronts and there the wind shifts are more immediate and more easily recognised. There are big lows and little lows and the more you come to recognise which kind is affecting you, the sooner you will be able to visualise your situation in the local wind scene and so come to divine what is likely to happen to the wind next. These abilities do not come easily. They require experience as well as knowledge, but as you acquire one you can acquire the other and so improve your tactical weather skills.

What kind of wind shifts you experience may depend very much on where you sail. I have divided up the sailing venues into those where people sail straight off the beach onto the open sea; where they sail just inland from a main sea coast; where they sail rather further inland and finally where they sail on elevated lakes and reservoirs or are generally enclosed by steep hill or mountain sides. Each of these zones will have its special wind systems of which, of the lowland venues, the coastal belt is the most likely to have local variations. However, it is the highland waters that have the most capricious winds and the most dangerous sudden storms so those who can take a board onto some previously virgin water high up between the hills or under the mountains must be warned of what to expect. By dividing the sailing areas into these zones I have been able to concentrate on their special problems, but sometimes what happens particularly in one zone will also, less often, happen in one or more of the others. Thus even if you do not habitually sail coastwise but are restricted to an inland body of water, it pays to read about weather and wind in other zones. Undoubtedly at some stage you will hope to sail on water other than those of 'home' and knowledge of their vagaries is important.

There are also local wind-shifters like thermal winds to be considered and such medium-scale wind systems are more susceptible to interpretation and action than many other weather phenomena. There are days when a seabreeze is inevitable and there are others where it takes a good deal of local knowledge to make up your mind what will happen. However, as the seabreeze is the coastal sailor's private wind it deserves close study. The warmer the clime then the more influence the seabreeze has on the local weather scene. The seabreeze is a good wind, providing enough strength to make the sailing interesting, but not to escalate the rate of capsizing.

Almost everyone is nonplussed by those periods of light airs which are close to calms. It always seems to be someone else who gets a private bit of wind and they run on, often into others who have no steerage way, only to lose it again while some other favourite of the wind gods is given a little gift of a zephyr. There are some pointers to where to find the lightest of light airs when it is apparently flat calm, but in this sphere you are often quite at the mercy of whatever local wind-making forces there may be.

Of more permanent help are the facts about how the wind acts in the lee of barriers to its progress. There are some pretty well-known bits of evidence to be had here which can be used to advantage by the denizens of river, lake and reservoir when caught in the inevitable lee of the trees or some other obstruction to air room. However, sometimes even here you cannot win. I once gave a lecture to a group of sailing enthusiasts who had all of Liverpool Bay to sail in and could not use it because at Southport, where they were, the tide ran out so far that fixtures on the sea were an impossibility. So they sailed on the artificial lake on the sea front. When the wind blew from certain directions, because there was an island in the lake there was just nowhere that you could sail between the lakeside and the island which was not in the zone of lowest wind speed. It is rare not to be able to escape the worst of the sheltering that comes from shoreside obstructions, but at Southport they really have a problem. Maybe you do too, because restrictions on water-space do not allow of the marks being laid clear of the lee of obstructions on many small lakes and reservoirs.

In this introduction I have mentioned some of the things that this book sets out to cover. They are the things which any small-boat sailor ought to know about the ways of the wind. However, there are more advanced techniques to be considered when the wind is variable and these you will want to study when you are experienced. The golden rule of beating to windward in variable winds is 'Tack on headers', that is when the wind heads you do not bear away, but tack. The more you sail variable winds the more you find that it is best not to follow this advice slavishly. The way the gradient and surface winds differ gives clues as to what shifts to expect and helps you sort out which headers to tack on and which ones to view with suspicion. The techniques may seem advanced, but they certainly help to make up the places.

I have introduced the 'polar performance diagram' here as the best way of sorting out tactics. This is because you can visualise the shape of the diagram for your craft and can then act accordingly. It is a great aid to getting the best out of your boat and is not, in my opinion, used half enough by small-craft sailors.

This introductory chapter has not mentioned all the aspects of wind and weather covered in the rest of the following chapters, but it is a beginning which leads us into forecasts and how they can help.

2 The Forecasts

Forecasters are trained as scientists, but they deal with an, as yet, rather unscientific subject – the weather. They are making great strides forward using the calculating power of massive computers to solve problems that once were insoluble to the practical forecaster. Yet even now they often cannot get the details of the forecast as right as many people would wish. Broadcast forecasts are brief and repetitive. The same story comes out in tantalisingly vague words and phrases hour after hour as you scan the air waves for something that will help you solve your problem of what the wind will do today.

The scheduled forecasts over the air are, in general, not aimed at coastal sailors. The land area forecasts are for the inland areas and cover vast tracts of land. The shipping forecasts are for the shipping fraternity and if they are of use to dinghy and board sailors then that is by accident and not design. These sea area forecasts are framed for ships on the deep sea and coastal conditions can be very different. You only have to live for a while on a sea coast – though not many of us do – to realise how the coastline often divides one kind of weather from another and this is particularly so in spring and autumn.

You can obtain the gist of the weather situation from the scheduled radio or TV forecasts and when the latter show charts they will give a good idea of how the situation is developing. Yet even when you know that fronts are coming in, or that a high is building across the country, you will still have to wait to see when the 'right-now' weather turns up. The small-boat sailor needs to know what the wind will be in the immediate hours not at some vague time in the future. But no forecast service will ever give him the information he needs with all the precise detail that would make the difference between making a tactically wrong decision and a right one. Even if we project forward into an uncertain future and assume that the Yacht Racing authorities permitted miniature radio receivers to be worn in every racing sailor's ear while an erudite met. genius fed them the latest information it would not revolutionise tactics overnight. We have to face the fact that the met. information that any dinghy or board sailor takes on the water with him will always be in his head. It will be the result of learning, allied to experience, and often formal meteorological knowledge is not going to help that process. Spectacular gains in races come from someone divining that a prevailing weather condition will produce a certain semi-permanent slant to the wind that is different from elsewhere and then actively seeking and using that knowledge. Or it comes about by accident and everyone follows the ones who were the lucky recipients of Lady Luck's help. However, if you have a good idea of why the wind has done what it has then you are in a better position to take advantage of the lift it may give you. No forecast service will be able to do that. You listen to what they have to say and use it as a skeleton on whose bones you will hang the flesh of the real conditions that obtain whenever and wherever you may be sailing.

That is why in this book there is just enough basic met. to help link the changes in wind direction together as pressure systems pass. It is of no use knowing the kind of meteorology that comes with an elementary or advanced pass in geography at school. That helps, but most of it is not of the faintest use to the practical sailor who wants to know what the wind will do next minute, or next hour. It is only changes in wind over relatively short periods plus the ability to see what conditions may be like for a race later today, or one tomorrow, that are worth knowing about. If formal met. helps that then formal met. is useful – otherwise it is only an encumbrance to hoisting in the important knowledge.

The wind at the surface is always being modified by thermal and topographic influences. So you need a reference wind that every forecaster will know about when you ring up for more information than you can get from the broadcast forecasts. That wind is called the 'gradient' wind because it follows along the isobars on the weather maps as if these were solid walls which it could not cross. Whenever you look at a weather chart then you will know which way the wind is blowing because the wind blows in the direction of the isobars and does so clockwise round Highs and anticlockwise round Lows in the Northern Hemisphere (NH). In the Southern Hemisphere (SH) the directions are reversed (Fig. 2.1).

Most people today are pretty aware of these facts so that they can see from a TV chart which way the wind is blowing without the presenters having to tell them. Anyway presenters often do not refer to the area you are interested in so you have to do it yourself by using your basic met. knowledge to move the whole situation on to the time and place you are interested in.

To this end you need to know that it is normal for all the world's weather to move from west to east. Around each hemisphere there is a merry-go-round of lows and highs drifting eastwards in the temperature latitudes, each going through its life-cycle and dying out only to be replaced by new embryonic pressure systems. Sometimes however this carousel of drifting weather is interrupted by the intervention of vast sprawling areas of high pressure. These so-called 'blocking' highs drive ridges of high pressure

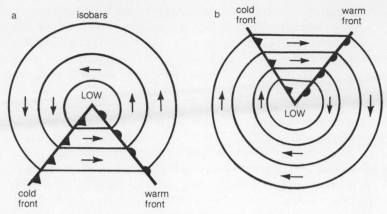

Figure 2.1 *How gradient winds blow round depressions in (a) the northern hemisphere and (b) the southern hemisphere*

like wedges up through the temperature latitudes and physically stop the eastward progress of the lows (Fig. 2.2).

Blocking highs produce those occasional phenomenal summers when almost constant fair weather occurs day after day for weeks and, in some cases, months on end. In winter they produce the equally phenomenal blizzards and Siberian white-outs that afflict latitudes that are used to more temperate conditions.

So apart from when highs block the east-going weather systems you can mentally move on the depressions and fronts etc. and so long as you do not expect to do it for more than twelve to twenty-four hours ahead you can often get a good idea of what tomorrow's picture will look like.

However, there is much more real information to be had which will help solve the problem of what the wind will be for tomorrow. This is to be found churning off the chart-drawing machines that are attached to the computers and which the Met. Offices will have to hand. When I was a forecaster the computer revolution was in its infancy and we were often very unsure of the correctness of our isobars for tomorrow. Today, with the help of the computers, the run of the isobars for tomorrow is pretty well known. Even for the next day they are quite reliable and for the day after that there is still a reasonable chance that what the computer says is the likely wind direction will indeed be so.

Thus, when you are race-planning it is as well to look up the local Public Service Met. Office in the telephone directory and ask them what the forecast surface charts look like for the time you are interested in. As the computers work ahead from today's raw observations, the forecasters feel they are moving towards some form of perfection. So much so that they are trying out forecasts of the isobaric patterns as far as six days ahead. Future developments may enable the broad outlines of the world's weather patterns

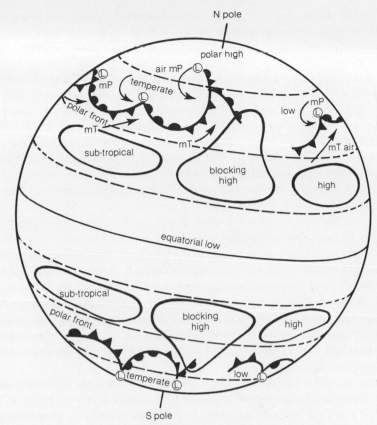

Figure 2.2 *The pressure belts of the world. While the sub-tropics are dominated by high pressure, a blocking high is shown diagrammatically in both hemispheres interrupting the flow of the westerlies*

to be predicted maybe weeks or months in in advance, but just for now having an idea of what the wind direction will be tomorrow and the next day is a great asset and is there for the cost of a phone call. Incidentally, these forecast charts come out at certain times of the day or the week (in the case of six-day forecasts) and it might also be worth asking, for future reference, when is the best time to ring.

When you are racing away from home why not ring the Public Service Met. Office nearest to the venue and see what they can tell you. They may well have forecasters working for them who are also sailors and will be able to talk your language – if you are prepared to talk theirs. It helps you and them immeasurably if you have done a bit of homework and actually know what the present situation is – you may even have seen a forecast chart on TV or in a newspaper and can then use that picture as a basis on which to hang the changes that their latest information will be giving them.

9

Obviously the nearer you ring to the time for which you want the information the more accurate it will be and you must not expect miracles when you ask what the wind will be over your creek or reservoir forty-eight hours hence.

It is the time that the weather features will arrive that is the most likely to be in error in a forecast and so windshifts due to fronts and the passage of depression centres are bound to be inaccurately timed. What you have to do here is to learn the wind changes that are normally expected when fronts pass, recognise the sky signs that go with the onset of fronts and troughs and then look for the immediate signs that say a shift is imminent. Then it is up to you to use your tactical ability to sort out the best move to make you windward boat after the shift has passed. Help with this is given in Chapter 16.

Because the met. men are not gods they can only advise on and point out weather features that are likely to upset or modify the wind over your sailing venue, but after that it is up to you to divine exactly when the changes will occur. The computers, for all their wonderful abilities with calculations, are not good at recognising the development of small local features. Thus small wave depressions often form on cold fronts and when your call to the forecaster at the Public Service office has revealed that a cold front will be crossing your area during the time you are racing, he may have no inkling that the whole picture can be very severely modified by the development of a wave.

You will expect a certain pattern of wind shifts to occur as the front passes and then for a different type of airstream to develop a new wind pattern, but when it comes to it the front seems to pass and you wait for the rain and cloud to clear – but it doesn't. You spend the rest of the race under leaden skies and sopping wet from the constant downpour when your met. knowledge led you to believe that the rain would tail off and the clouds lift – which is what the textbooks say! The wind may shift back again for quite a time before the eventual clearance comes, but in the interim the race is over and you are towelling down in the clubhouse or even home in bed.

I have just picked out a weather feature that is of constant occurrence and which gives forecasters more headaches than almost any other (forecasting the arrival or clearance of sea fog is perhaps even more difficult), but it is not the only unheralded disturber of the weather scene that will make the forecast very wrong from a sailing point of view.

If the wind is forecast to be SW and it comes in from S then you do not complain. Weather is like that, but if you find the wind is E when it was forecast as being SW than that raises the hackles. When these things happen the wind is often not very strong, but when you have thought out how you intend to sail a race and the wind comes in from the almost diametrically opposite direction then you feel you have reason for complaint.

If this should happen suspect that a small low centre has developed and that it is somewhere south of you. Then use your knowledge of cyclonic wind changes (page 61) to forecast for yourself what the wind should do. Of course a phone call could establish this, but maybe you have no change or even time to worry about such niceties. The wind is east – so be it.

It is usually small pressure systems which develop without warning that produce winds from directions unheralded by any forecast and so the weather signs should be there as well. If you learn to recognise the cloud patterns that go with local depressions then you will be in a better situation to divine what wind shifts should be coming along in the next few hours.

These are cogent reasons for knowing about weather when you sail a dinghy or a board. Racing becomes ever more competitive and people become ever more adept at stealing marches on their competitors. After all the work has been done on hulls and rigs and the right suit of sails, you then have your acquired ability to sail the boat, your knowledge of the rules, the tidal streams and the tactical things you ought to do to make the best way to windward: head across the wind or run before it. However, there is one other last frontier to be crossed and that is to acquire a more and more intimate knowledge of what makes and shifts the wind. There is a vast untapped area of know-how here just waiting to be explored, mapped and used. I personally have spent quite a long time sorting out what is useful knowledge for dinghy sailors from the morass of meteorology that may occupy met. courses for other sailors such as Yachtmasters etc. Most of that knowledge which is useful to dinghy and board sailors is in the following pages, but you always need a reference direction for the wind to hang the changes on. That reference is the gradient wind which needs a little explanation.

3 Gradient Wind, Isobars and Weather Maps

Whatever the wind does at the surface, the wind at about 2000 feet up goes on blowing in the same direction as it did before. It changes in the way we see the rings of isobars change on the weather maps, but it is not affected by normal terrain nor by thermal influences like land and seabreezes. Great mountain barriers obviously stand in the way of wind which we assume is a relatively small distance above our heads, but for the majority who will be sailing small waters, coastwise or inland, the definition that the gradient wind is the wind blowing at about 2000 feet up is good.

Meteorologists have chosen the round figure of 2000 feet because most surface effects do not reach up that high, and it happens to be convenient. We shall speak later about turbulent eddies in the wind, but for the most part, until you are getting on for gale force winds, these do not grow big enough to affect the gradient wind. The bubbles of heated air we call thermals go this high and higher and when they reveal their presence by forming puffs of cumulus (Cu) cloud over themselves these drift along in the gradient wind. In fact when you see Cu clouds moving then you are looking at the speed and direction of the gradient wind.

The surface wind will nearly always be different from the gradient, but all the frictional collisions that modify the wind near the surface do not affect the gradient wind as it sails along above you. This is why I have introduced a wind that you cannot reach or feel as being the most important reference wind you can know about. It might be advisable to briefly explain the name 'gradient' wind.

If the earth did not spin, weather would not be anything like we know it. Wind would blow directly from high pressure to low pressure and none of the dartboard rings of isobars would be seen on weather maps. Wind actually does this near the equator, but tropical meteorology is a special subject that will not be covered here. This book is about temperate latitude wind and weather where the spin of the earth has a big effect on the way winds blow.

If wind did blow from high to low pressure directly it would be as if it were flowing down a pressure hill. The contours of a pressure 'hill' are the isobars and just as if a ball were rolled downhill the steeper the gradient of the isobars the stronger the wind. Effects due to the earth's rotation (that we need not go into) do not allow the wind to flow straight down the gradient, but deflect it to the right of its path in the NH (to the left in the SH) until it ends up blowing not down the gradient, but along it. The situation is rather akin to a 'wall-of-death' rider who balances gravity downwards against centrifugal force and so rides round the 'contours' of the wall. For the gradient wind it is pressure forces that replace gravity and the earth's spin provides the centrifugal force, in this case called the geostrophic force (see Figs. 11.1 and 11.2).

Despite the fact that the gradient wind blows round lows and highs (and not directly from high pressure to low) it is still a fact that the steeper the gradient of the isobars (that is, the closer they appear on a weather map) the stronger the wind has got to be to balance the tendency it has to 'fall' in towards low pressure. This follows because the geostrophic force increases with wind speed. Here is an explanation of the fact that 'tight' isobars mean strong wind while widely-spaced isobars mean light winds (Fig. 3.1). In the

Figure 3.1 *Features of the weather map and the idea that closely-spaced isobars go with strong winds and vice versa. The short arrows show how surface winds blow compared to the gradient wind (long arrows)*

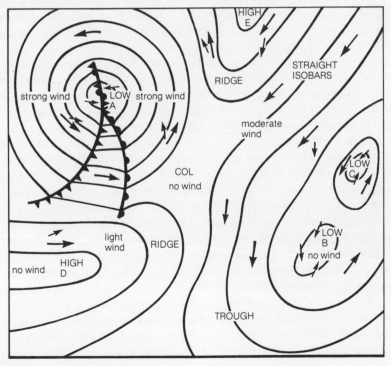

middle of highs and lows where the isobars make closed rings there will therefore be no wind. We expect this with highs because we associate highs with light conditions, but it is also useful to realise that when a low centre tracks over you there will be a temporary 'eye-of-the-storm' experience with next to no wind for a time and then the wind will pick up from an entirely different direction to the one it had before the calm.

Thus the gradient wind has some important attributes:

  i it blows to keep Low pressure on its Left (NH).
 ii it blows within the confines of the isobars.
iii the closer the isobars the stronger the wind.

In Fig. 3.1. the heavy arrows represent the gradient wind while the lighter arrows show typical directions for the surface wind. We see here how surface winds spiral out of highs into lows. This figure also introduces some features of the weather map.

A col is the 'saddle-backed' pressure region between two lows and two highs.
A ridge is a high pressure extension of an anticyclone.
A trough is a low pressure extension of a depression.

Weather improves in ridges and deteriorates in troughs. There may be no front in a trough, but whatever weather occurs it is always worse than elsewhere. Showers intensify in number and size in troughs and may even develop so much local cloud as to look like a front. Such air-mass troughs are mentioned again on page 22.

Wherever a run of isobars is straight the weather remains fairly constant in type for as long as the straight isobars stay over the area, but directly they begin to develop a bulge away from low pressure, that is when a trough appears, the cloud increases, the chance of rain or snow increases and the general trend is to poorer weather. On the other hand if the isobars bulge away from high pressure (and they are always wriggling about one way and then the other) what was not so good weather improves as the sky breaks or even clears and any tendency to rain dies away. Showers are rare in such ridges and we say the weather is 'anticyclonic' in type whereas when a minor (or even a major) trough appears it is said to be 'cyclonic'.

We see the kinks in the isobars along the fronts in Fig. 3.1. are away from low pressure and so along these fronts there are troughs. They are frontal troughs (as opposed to non-frontal troughs) and if the isobars suddenly change direction then so too will the wind when the front passes. Conversely, when a sprawling ridge edges over there will be wind shifts, but they will be slow and sometimes almost imperceptible.

If frontal symbols are not familiar let me make it clear that warm fronts have warm knobs on while cold fronts have cold ice spikes. The amalgamation of the two symbols shows an occluded front. The symbols are always on the side towards which the front is moving so that the occlusion to the north of the centre of Low A is moving in the opposite direction to the part to the south.

I mentioned anticyclones that block the paths of the lows and are called 'blocking highs' for this reason. It is they who bring long periods of good weather. The cyclonic equivalents are the quasi-stationary lows and very often these look like Lows B and C. Just like a pair of prize fighters they gyrate round each other, but do not go anywhere and if you should be within their compass then the weather can remain poor and cyclonic for days or even weeks. Low A may look worse, but it is often mobile and could cancel the racing today, but be gone by tomorrow.

4 The Surface Wind

It is a remarkable fact that were it not for the frictional drag of the land and sea on the winds in depressions they could never fill up. Attribute (ii) of the gradient wind (page 14) would keep the wind always blowing in closed paths and would never allow air to flow into the centre of lows so that they could feed the rising currents that are their life-support system.

Looked at overall, a depression is a region where more air is rising than is sinking while an anticyclone is a region where more air is sinking than rising. Now if air comes down from very high up it has to splay out over the ground just as you project water from a hosepipe onto the ground. Thus anticyclones are the agents by which air at great altitude is brought down to the surface while depressions return the air to altitude. However, unless the air could flow across the isobars out of high and into low pressure the interchange would soon cease. Thus the surface wind is always blowing at an angle across the isobars from the high pressure side to the low one.

The angles that the surface winds make with the gradient wind above depend on how rough the surface is over which they travel. Thus over the sea the surface wind blows in towards low pressure at an average angle of about 15° while over the land it doubles this to about 30° (Fig. 4.1.).

Now having said this, these are only average values and sometimes the values are less and sometimes more. As this is an introductory chapter we will leave the factors that vary the angles to a later chapter.

Note that for the SH the surface wind acts just as in the NH, but in the opposite sense, that is, if you stood looking along the direction of the isobars (the gradient wind direction), then the surface wind would come slightly from your left in the SH whereas it comes from your right in the NH.

In practice of course it is the surface wind in which we sail and which therefore becomes our reference wind direction. We have to do a little thinking and visualising to see what the gradient wind must be doing. However, let us take an example.

The wind is blowing from W and you sail a reservoir or other body of inland water which is set in rolling, but not very elevated land. How do you find the gradient wind direction? Stand with your back to the wind and then rotate clockwise by 30° (anticlockwise in the SH). You will then be looking

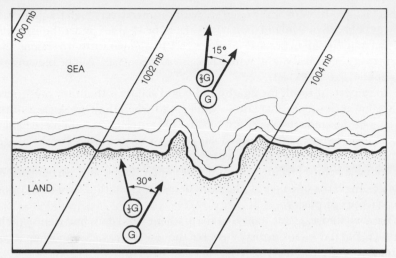

Figure 4.1 *The average angles between gradient wind and surface wind in the northern hemisphere. If (G) is the gradient wind speed then the fractions shown will be the average speed of the surface wind*

along the direction of the gradient wind. If you are on the coast and the wind is blowing straight off the sea then rotate through 15°, but realise that a very short run over land may easily shift the direction to 20° to 30° and time of day and even time of year can have a profound effect on how big the angular difference is between the gradient and the surface wind. However, note that while the wind direction will shift as it moves from a smooth surface like the sea to a rough one like the land (or vice versa) the gradient wind will blow in exactly the same direction over adjacent land and sea. It is for this reason that we choose the gradient wind as the reference direction and not the much more variable surface wind. Further, when you see a weather map and have to gauge the wind direction from the isobars it is the gradient wind direction you will be looking at and you will have to mentally shift the direction across the isobars to find the truer surface direction.

Because direction is more important than speed in racing we concentrated on that, but because of surface friction the gradient wind is normally stronger than the surface wind. When forecasting wind speed the met. men measure the speed of the gradient wind from the isobars because there is a simple relationship between their distance apart and the gradient wind speed. They allow for how curved the isobars may be (as very tightly curved isobars go with a lowered wind speed) and then they divide the gradient speed by three. The surface wind overland they take to be a third of the gradient speed and they double this (two thirds of the gradient speed) over the sea.

It is for this reason that it is very rare to have gale-force winds over land whereas gales blow over the open sea with comparatively high frequency. If you get Force 8 or 9 inland then it is Force 10 or 11 at sea under the same run of isobars. Equally, because of the effect of temperature inversions that form over the land at night, it may be calm at the surface, but be blowing say at 20 knots at 2000 feet.

An important result for dinghy and board sailors is that they must make due allowance for the increase in wind speed when they break clear of the shelter of the land. If you are not too sure of yourself, your ability to handle the craft in twice the wind speed you have, or of your crew (in the case of dinghies), then keep under the lee of the land. Stay in the creeks and be sure of yourself before pushing out into more open waters and particularly do not go out on the open sea at a harbour or estuary mouth. It can be the most treacherous of places.

We shall find at a later stage that the gradient wind does find its way to the surface, but it does so on gusty days and the results are very important if you intend to make the most of variable wind patterns.

5 Forecast Terms

The words that appear in forecasts can have a deeper meaning than appears at first sight. Here are some of the words and phrases interpreted in the interests of sailing.

Terms Used for Daytime Conditions

Sunny	sunshine most of the time.	days when thermal winds will be most in evidence. Winds often variable.
Sunny periods	more sunshine than cloud.	winds are often variable and Force 4 or less.
Sunny intervals	more cloud than sunshine.	winds are sometimes strong with this airstream. It can be muggy.
Bright	diffuse sun through high cloud. Some direct sun.	old fronts and coming fronts produce bright skies. Look for a wind shift later.
Bright periods	bright sky for over half the time.	again fronts are often to blame. Can be thundery soon.
Bright intervals	brief bright periods, otherwise cloudy.	not a very pleasant day.
Cloudy	cloud covers most of the sky for most of the time.	can be associated with both cyclonic and anticyclonic weather.
Dull	dark cover of cloud – less light than with cloudy.	centres of depressions and cyclonic weather generally, but also found with fronts that have come from industrial smoke regions.
Fine	no precipitation or thick fog. Some sunshine.	can be sunny periods or intervals or bright. Covers many a day's weather.
Dry	as above but no sunshine.	sky is overcast but it will not rain.

When There will be Some Precipitation

Rain	precipitation in the form of water drops. Often starts lightly and increases with time.	most rain is from warm fronts and occlusions, so you can expect a veering wind shift later (backing SH).

Continuous rain	rain goes on for some hours without much respite.	the rainfall from virile fronts which are fairly young and so fully active. Can also come from troughs of low pressure.
Intermittent rain	periods of rain longer than dry periods between.	old fronts or occluded fronts often produce this rainfall type.
Occasional rain	dry periods longer than the periods of rain.	this is not 'showers' although in brief forecasts it may be described as such. The rain is not as heavy as with showers and no clear intervals occur. Again it is usually an old front but one that is weaker than above.
Thundery rain	occasional or intermittent rain which varies in intensity but heavy at times. Usually but not necessarily accompanied by thunder.	odd days from a wind point of view. Sometimes very little and at others quite squally puffs. May develop into full-blooded thunderstorms. Often a front has become unstable after a hot period. Expect Force 3–5 from a new direction when it has passed.
Showers	heavy bursts of rain for a short time. The rain starts suddenly and usually ends suddenly.	there are clearing skies between true showers, but many situations where rain is intermittent are described as showers due to lack of air-time to describe the real situation. Quite big tactical wind shifts occur with showers (see page 34).
Thundery showers	showers of rain, hail, sleet or snow, usually heavy and accompanied by thunder.	these are the heaviest kind of showers other than those which occur with thunderstorms. Squally gusts occur near their edges, but wind sinks in speed as they pass (see page 35).
Thunderstorms	thunder and lightning with or without precipitation which may be continuous over a considerable period and heavy at times.	the most prodigious showers occur with storms. Gusts up to 40 knots may occur. Tornadoes appear inland with some of the worst storms and waterspouts at sea. The risk of dinghies and boards being struck is small (see page 141).
Drizzle	periods with very small raindrops falling at high density.	drizzle may seem like rain, but the situation for drizzle is different. Drizzle can occur from thick low clouds. Rain needs deep clouds. Coastal drizzle comes with mT air (see page 64). In highland venues long periods of drizzle occur when it is dry on the lowlands. Visibility is poor in drizzle.
Hail	ice spheres from deep cumulonimbus clouds.	hail in the forecast means heavy showers, squalls and possibly

		thunder. There will be semi-permanent windshifts as the big showers or storms pass.
Snow	flakes of ice crystals when lower air is cold.	late autumn into spring is snow time in temperate latitudes. Visibility and morale fall rapidly in snow showers. No snow sailing without a suit.

How Certain is the Forecast?

When as a forecaster you deal with an uncertain thing like the weather it is essential to give the public an idea of how sure you are of what you are saying.

Thus the met. services tend to use three to four degrees of confidence which are going to be something like the following:

First degree of confidence	there are no qualifying words or phrases.	it *will* be mainly cloudy today.
Second degree of confidence	words like 'probably', 'likely', 'expected to', etc. appear in the forecast.	it is *probable* that another depression will follow this one in from the Atlantic. Rain is *expected to* spread from the west reaching the east by evening.
Third degree of confidence	words like 'prospect of', 'indications of', etc. appear in the forecast.	there is *every prospect* that the rain will clear the region during the afternoon. There are *indications of* a small wave depression forming on this cold front.
Fourth degree	words like 'may', 'chance of', 'risk of', 'possibly' and 'perhaps' creep into the forecast.	there is a *chance* that thunderstorms may break out tomorrow afternoon. There is the *risk of* showers breaking out over higher ground. The low centre may *possibly* turn and track north.

Confidence Tricks

If you listen to the forecasts it may seem rather remarkable how confident they sound about tomorrow's weather. However, when you then come down to thinking about what the conditions will really be like for a race or just a spin, you find you do not know as much about it as you would like.

Whatever you may think, forecasters hate being imprecise. When forecasting for military or civil aircraft they can be very precise for most of the time. This is because they are in constant touch with the crews who are using the information and the crews themselves are half way to being meteorologists. Neither of these things obtain when the forecasts are designed for the general public. The public are not at all met.-minded and from this point of view the sailing fraternity are not the general public. The sailing recipients for the most part are well able to take advantage of more detailed information couched in more imprecise terms than the general public are. Yet the forecasts over radio and TV must be written with the general public in mind.

Thus the forecasters have had to come to a compromise that they do not really like. They have been forced to be imprecise about timing the weather so that they can sound more precise about the overall situation. This is well illustrated by showery situations.

When an unstable airstream comes down across the country then at most times of year there are showers. So when the upper air soundings (that are taken twice a day at many points throughout the world) show that the air is set up to erupt into showers, the forecast will say 'Tomorrow *will* be showery'. That high degree of confidence is warranted because certainly there will, over the large areas which the forecasts cover, be showers. However, the probability that you personally will experience showers may be quite low. You may be in a shower-shadow where, because showers have been particularly intensified by being forced over a hill ridge which is upwind of you, there could be few if any showers. You may not lie in the path of any of the showers that occur and so while showers could be occurring all round you, you personally will not experience one.

Now that is not exactly a con trick. It is the forecasters doing their best to warn ordinary mortals that they may get wet and to take a mac or an umbrella. But sailing people are not ordinary mortals when it comes to weather. The shower that comes along when you can just lay the turning mark, and which shifts the wind at the last moment so that you cannot do so, may lose you a commanding lead or at least a place in the prizes.

However, as showers are impossible to forecast in exact time and place, so the forecast that says 'There will be showers tomorrow', which sounds like the highest degree of confidence, leaves you not much wiser than before.

In any event it is very unusual for showers to occur one after another from morning to night. Sometimes you get a shower in the morning and then not another one until after lunch. Some people not far from you may not have any showers at all, or they may find they get one late in the afternoon which you miss entirely. Sometimes the showers concentrate into lines of shower clouds stretched across the wind that look like a cold front. However, it is useful to be able to recognise that such a nasty-looking line is not in fact a front at all, but what is called an 'air-mass trough'.

With an air-mass trough the weather both before and behind is much the same. From a tactical sailing point of view the wind backs (NH) (veers SH) by a moderate degree ahead of the passage of the trough and veers behind (backs SH). There will be squally gusts associated with the showers as the rain falls, but it usually all passes in less than an hour.

You recognise air-mass troughs more by place and time than anything else. You will not find them on coasts facing the wind, nor will they organise greatly before a considerable amount of land has been traversed. They are to be expected in the forenoon and afternoon of days that promise to be showery, but away from the coasts onto which the wind is blowing. For example, when I was forecasting weather in the middle reaches of the South Coast of England we came to recognise the 'one o'clock trough' as we called it, because on showery days with a NW wind a band of showers would march down upon us at about lunch-time. Now that I live further east the trough comes as a 'two o'clock trough', illustrating that the phenomenon traverses the country, occurring later as it travels southeastwards.

Such troughs will not usually be mentioned in forecasts, but they make quite a difference to sailing weather because often, as if the trough were a sort of vacuum-cleaner, it sweeps the sky ahead of it clear of cloud as well as the air behind and so no shower has a chance to grow other than along the trough-line itself.

Now it is not the forecasters' fault that these oddities in a showery airstream are not mentioned. They could not give the detail required other than to say that a band of showers might cross the area sometime during the early afternoon. They are not given the time to provide anything other than the broadest outline of the weather and it is a constant problem to them as to how best to convey the tenor of the weather as well as its content.

More stations are getting weather radars and if you were able to ring one of those they would be tracking the showers and would be able to tell you where the showers were. However, a shower is not a sort of aerial fountain that can go on deluging water onto the ground for ever more. There is only so much water-vapour in a cloud and when that is used up the shower dies out. The cloud from which it fell does not immediately disappear, but the falling winds that went with the falling water die out and so gusts become less violent. In this way showers grow, travel and die to be replaced by others. A shower may seem a constant thing when you are static, but if you were able to travel a motorway keeping a shower overhead all the time you would then be able to notice its life-cycle. Like most 'right-now' weather you have to learn to recognise the signs and know what normally happens so that you can be ready to react to it the moment it arrives.

Let us take another example at the other end of the scale. The airstream is a little unstable, but it is touch and go whether the ground temperature will get high enough to produce thermals strong enough to produce showers. Any form of uplift can however change that situation and make the air unstable so wherever there are hills, showers may occur. In such areas showers can grow big and frequent while everywhere else it is quite fair. The forecast will try to indicate that some people will experience showers, but that the majority will remain dry. Only you can know your own terrain well enough to divine what risk there is for your sailing waters. The trouble is that the difference in wind speed between areas with no showers and the gusts that come with the onset of showers will be very marked. It could be generally 10 knots in sunny regions and rise to 20 or more knots in the showers. People learning to sail boards for example would find it easy and pleasant in a 10-knot wind under sunny skies, but impossible in twice that wind speed under a deluge of cold rain.

The fact is that when the first degree of confidence word 'will' appears in the forecast it always leaves the small-boat sailor with a problem of exactly when the weather will arrive. It almost certainly 'will' come, but if it is scheduled for the afternoon say, it could come early in a race or be delayed until everyone is ashore. You cannot time weather that accurately except when you are following it on a weather radar. The only radar you have is your eyes which see the clouds approaching. It is then a question of recognising what is about to happen and acting accordingly.

One further important example could be covered. When the isobars bend anticyclonically then air sinks from very high up. Sinking air warms up by compression and warmth produced this way spells death to clouds at altitude and so also to any prospects of rain. However, sometimes this 'subsidence' (officially pronounced sub*sid*ence) is not quite strong enough to rub out all the rain and, because the forecasters do not have enough information to recognise that subsidence is going to occur, what was a forecast of a considerable amount of rain turns out to be just a smattering of light rain or the rain becomes intermittent when it was expected to be continuous.

If the anticyclonic effect is very marked it can become totally blue sky and no matter how hot it gets no clouds appear. Temperatures in summer then reach record levels and no shading clouds appear to temper the heat. The only cool place to be is on the water, but the winds are sluggish and even seabreezes, which you might think with all this warmth should be strong, hardly appear.

Figure 5.1 *The two kinds of inversion layer that occur near the ground: (a) is the overnight inversion that sets in most nights and (b) is a subsidence inversion that only occurs in certain anticyclonic situations*

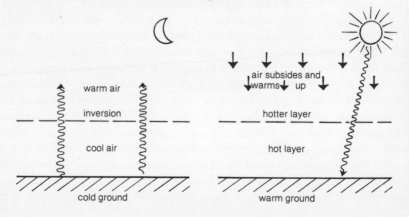

It is all due to a 'subsidence inversion' squatting near the ground – a layer so warmed by compression that no thermals can punch through it (Fig. 5.1).

The semi-permanent high that settles over the Central and Eastern Mediterranean in summer is an example where a subsidence inversion remains day after sweltering day and no matter to what heights the surface temperature rises it just stays completely cloudless.

Thus, while the normal forecasts will never mention them, it is useful to recognise that there are two classes of inversion layer that form just above the sailing layer:

i the overnight inversion that occurs most nights and can be broken during the day to create more wind, and
ii the subsidence inversion that occurs in anticyclonic weather and often cannot be broken so that winds remain sluggish throughout the day.

Winds on either occasion might be described as 'light and variable', but the sequence of events described under 'The Wind's Day' (Chapter 10) will occur with the overnight inversion, not with the subsidence inversion.

6 Looking at the Sky

Clouds

If you intend to make any sense out of the weather and so interpret the wind changes that go with it, you have to become conversant with certain cloud types. Of all clouds the most easily recognised perhaps is the cotton-wool heap cloud called *cumulus* (Cu). It is also the one you will find most often referred to in this book. This is because it usually populates the sky in fair weather. It is the cloud of the world's oceans because on average the sea is a degree or two warmer than the air over it. Having said which, there will be many times when Cu is not present in the daytime sky. However, this will usually be when one or other of the following situations occur:

 i there is a layer of high cloud that cuts off the sun and so inhibits the thermal currents that generate Cu. This is often the case when a warm front or occlusion is approaching.
 ii there is an inversion near the ground which prevents thermals rising to a height where the moisture in them can cool and condense into Cu. This is the situation in the mornings and evenings of fair weather.
 iii the air is over a cool sea surface which prevents convection occurring. This needs a coastal venue and an on-shore wind direction.
 iv there are sinking currents near the surface as happens when seabreezes become established. This occurs over the coasts and leads to hours of sunshine when inland it is quite cloudy.

Cumulus is the cloud of an airstream which has wind shifts in it that can be in some way predicted and used to advantage. It may very well grow large and so lead to showers in which case it becomes *cumulonimbus* (Cb). The largest forms of Cb will grow anvil tops and are associated with thunderstorms. As *nimbus* means 'rain-bearing' so any heap cloud that produces showers can be recognised as a cumulonimbus.

Heaps are one of the two main shapes that clouds adopt. The other is a layer form called *stratus* or, when prefixing other cloud names, *strato-*. Thus a well-known cloud type which consists of globular masses covering large areas of the sky is called *stratocumulus* (Sc), that is, a layer of heaps.

Once you see how the cloud names are constructed these become easier to remember. Meteorologists recognise many forms of clouds, but we can simplify the types into three height decks: high, medium level and low, plus two cloud types that span these height decks.

Recognising cloud height is a very skilled business and even quite experienced observers will argue about the height of an individual cloud. Small-craft sailors do not have to worry about such niceties. It is usually fairly easy to see if one cloud is higher than another or, if they exist on their own in the sky, either their characteristic shape or how high they look will usually give the cloud type.

The highest clouds in the sky are so cold as to be composed of ice crystals. These are the cirrus clouds of which there are three kinds:

Cirrus (Ci) looking like skeins of white hair or like hooks.

Cirrostratus (Cs) a layer of ice-crystal cloud forming ring haloes about the sun or the moon.

Cirrocumulus (Cc) islands or rafts of minute globules which are very rarely seen so can be forgotten for our purposes.

Cirrus and cirrostratus are very well worth learning to recognise as they tell of coming warm fronts and occlusions. Thus they warn excellently of deteriorating weather and also a cyclonic wind-shift pattern as described on page 61.

Clouds that occupy the airspace between low and high clouds, that is to say medium clouds, have names that are prefixed alto-. There are the heap varieties – *altocumulus* (Ac) – and the layer varieties – *altostratus* (As).

Altostratus blots out the sun as the wedge of cloud that forms on a warm front or occlusion moves in. However, technically As cannot produce rain. To the earthbound observer the grey layer that produces rain may look no different from the grey layer that does not, but if thick dirty-looking layer clouds produce rain then they are called *nimbostratus* (Ns) and here we see the 'rain-bearing' word being used as a prefix whereas with the heap cloud that produces showers (cumulonimbus) it is a suffix.

This is of no consequence. What is important is that both the 'nimbus' clouds stretch up through the atmosphere through thousands of feet so that they can between them produce almost all the rain we get. Continuous rain falls from Ns whereas showery rain falls from Cb – the former produces most of the rain and snow in the winter half of the year while the latter contributes most to summer rainfall.

Having described the high clouds, the medium clouds and the two rain-bearing clouds that span the height categories, we are left with the low clouds of which we have already described cumulus and stratocumulus. Which really only leaves *stratus* (St). Stratus comes in many forms, but it is the low fog-like cloud that sometimes settles onto local hills and may at times come almost to ground level. It is often associated with drizzle especially in highland venues. Other forms of stratus are called 'fracto-stratus' or 'scud' that hangs wisp-like below clearing fronts and the type which is called 'pannus', which forms in rain that falls from Ns cloud and constitues the apparent cloud-base during the rainy phases of bad weather.

We can sum up the major forms of clouds in a simple table:

High clouds	Cirrus Ci	fibrous ice-crystal clouds which often foretell coming bad weather.
	Cirrostratus Cs	a thin veil of white cloud, often covering most of the sky and in which ring haloes form.
	Cirrocumulus Cc	small globular masses that may easily be mistaken for small Ac.
Medium-level clouds	Altostratus As	grey, often featureless layer clouds into which the sun disappears as if going behind ground glass.
	Altocumulus Ac	rafts or islands of globular masses usually larger than those seen in Cc.
Low clouds	Stratus St	low amorphous layer cloud covering the whole sky and associated with drizzle and poor visibility.
	Cumulus Cu	small heap clouds that may however grow into Cb.
	Stratocumulus Sc	layers of globular elements often covering large areas of the sky.
Rain-bearing clouds	Nimbostratus Ns	the layer cloud of bad weather that produces continuous rain – a frontal cloud.

Cumulonimbus Cb   the heap cloud that produces showers and thunderstorms – may or may not be associated with fronts.

7 Wind Shifts in the Sky

It will become very evident to the reader of this book that I have a limited belief in the usefulness of weather forecasts for dinghy and board sailors. What you must do is to have the gist of the weather situation in your mind before you go afloat and use it as a prop on which to hang your immediate recognition of the wind shifts that are coming your way. That means gaining experience of what skies produce what effects.

Dark foreboding skies usually mean dark foreboding weather, but what will the wind do? That, for small-waters sailors, is the only truly important question compared to which all other weather problems pale into insignificance. Will the wall of cloud you see coming make any difference to the wind you now have, or will it not? The wall may possibly be a front or the axis of a trough of low pressure. It may be just that the cloud has come down from an industrial area and is engorged with smoke so it looks much worse than it is. On the other hand if thunder rumbles from the direction of the dark line of cloud heading your way then you allow for the worst and if it is not a matter of tremendous gravity like a race you must win or gain points in, you would be advised to pull up on the shore somewhere. For under the dark roll-cloud of a thunderstorm the wind can be very vicious and powerful indeed.

When it has been a dreary, but hard-fought flog around the buoys in the steady downpour and the latter has, to your knowledge, been going on for some hours you will come to expect that a warm front must be imminent. So the rain, because of its consistency and duration, tells you that the break you see coming from windward is a warm front and you will expect a veering shift as it passes (backing in SH).

Here are reasons for knowing the way fronts behave so that the wind shifts they bring can be recognised before they occur. Warm front wind shifts are not normally as sharp or as certain as those that come with cold fronts, but there is far longer warning. You often have warning from a forecast that a cold front is imminent and then you can be more sure that the dirty-looking line of cloud on the horizon is the front which is going to produce squalls and another veer of wind (again back in the SH).

The problem with weather and its recognition is that there are always complications that blur nice simple pictures. When depressions are getting on in their life cycle they occlude. That means the cold front overtakes the warm front and what were two fronts merge into one. Ahead of the occlusion it looks like a warm front, behind it looks like a cold front and there is dark cloud, sometimes, but not always, with trailing wisps of scud beneath it to mark where what was the warm front changes, without a break, into the cold front. However, the wind shift may be under that line or the total shifts may have been going on, as a set of smaller shifts, for several hours.

The occlusion is a very prevalent kind of front when depressions have moved a long way from their normal breeding grounds. In Europe those grounds are the wastes of the North Atlantic and many fronts that cross Britain and Atlantic Europe are occlusions. On the eastern seaboard of the USA the breeding ground may be over the middle of Canada and the occlusion process may or may not be very advanced as the lows track out into the Atlantic.

It is these complications that put many sailing people off learning about weather. The only advice I can offer is to learn the most important things and let the rest come later.

Fronts and their recognition are important, but so also are small depressions that track through an area and shift the wind about in certain ways depending on where you are with respect to the low centre. Only wind direction coupled to the history of the weather you have just experienced can provide a clear picture of where you are with respect to the moving centre and what therefore must subsequently happen.

For example, you troubled to find out that a cold front was in the offing and now you have been subjected to a constant downpour for an hour or more and the rain has been occasionally heavy so that visibility has been cut quite dramatically. Before the rain came along it seemed warm, but now there is a chill in the air. You, rightly, suspect that this is the cold front you were warned of and you know that clearing skies follow the passage of such a front. So you are looking for the clearance. The wind, which has been from a point south of west, is now stuck firmly in the northwest and it all points to the cold front clearing. Indeed, you can see the lighter sky coming over the horizon to windward. It will soon be pleasanter sailing (Fig. 7.1a).

Then, much to your disbelief, the clearance you could see has disappeared and the rain goes on. Not as hard as previously, but still hard enough (Fig. 7.1b). It continues to rain for the next couple of hours and then wonder-of-wonders the cold front you saw so tantalisingly approaching two saturated hours ago clears and the sun comes out (Fig. 7.1c).

What you have experienced is the passage of a wave in the cold front and Fig. 7.1. shows you what happens and what wind shifts are likely to come along when it does happen. Waves are very prevalent and may appear on both warm and cold fronts although they are experienced more with the latter than the former. They may be such small ripples in the otherwise smooth cold front that only those like dinghy and board sailors, who need to meet every shift in the wind, need ever notice them.

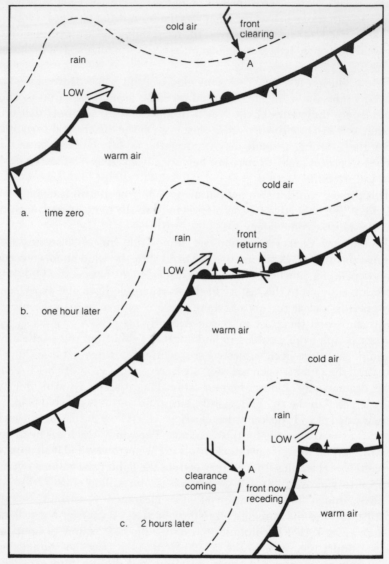

Figure 7.1 *How a wave low spoils what looked like a clearing situation.*
(a) You are assumed to be at A and the front is moving in the directions and with the relative speeds indicated by the arrows. As the front is moving back so in (b) you have low cloud and rain again (maybe thunder in summer). It may take several hours to get to situation (c) where the front finally clears

However, it is as well to realise that most depressions start off as small waves in the Polar Front (Chapter 13) and develop into full-scale systems. This cyclogenesis as it is called may be going on over you when you experience the adverse weather of a wave. The essential difference between the wave that is going to grow into a depression and the one which will merely slip along the cold front, like a hump flicked into a partly taut rope, is speed of clearance.

The little travelling wave is gone in a few hours or less, but the developing depression may stay with you for twelve or more hours before it moves on. It is as well to find out about the climatology of your own area to see if yours is one of the places where lows habitually form, especially as the areas which breed lows may not always seem to be the most likely. The Cote d'Azur is renowned for its weather and yet the Gulf of Genoa next door is one of the favourite breeding grounds for depressions in the Mediterranean. In another continent entirely we find that many of the lows that sweep down across the eastern Atlantic states of the USA are born over Alberta. For Britain and Atlantic Europe it is the Atlantic in whose nest the atmosphere rears its young depressions and the same for the Western seaboard of North America as the lows develop over the North Pacific.

In essence what all these examples show is that the intelligence on the next wind shift will usually be written in the clouds if you are able to read the message. To this end let me set down a few well-tried principles:

i Change in high clouds warns of wind change many hours in advance.
ii Change in medium-level clouds may give warning of wind shifts some hours in advance or the change may come more rapidly depending on the kind of cloud involved.
iii Change in low clouds spells immediate change in wind. You may not know exactly what change to expect, but you are ready for something new when the rift in the cloudiness or the darker line in an otherwise featureless cloudbase bears down on you.

The above is seen to lead to this:

The higher the clouds that appear the longer is the warning of wind change at the surface and conversely the lower the clouds the shorter the warning.

The reverse may not be the case because often the wind shift has already occurred when high clouds break and disappear. An important example that springs to mind is when a cold front is clearing and the high clouds along its trailing edge lift and recede. The wind shift occurred possibly as long as two to three hours ago. Yet even here, as the sun comes out on land previously in shadow, convection currents build and so do heap clouds which immediately changes the kind of wind you have from a more-or-less steady one to one full of shifts and gusts.

You can actually see this happening. When it has rained and then stopped and to windward you can see the clear-cut lines of cloud breaking as if cut with a knife into blue sky then you will normally also see a blue corridor that brings you into sunshine for say half an hour or so before cumulus clouds begin to build. The wider the blue corridor behind the frontal cloud the faster the latter is travelling and conversely if you can see big tops thrusting up into the edge of the clearing front it is very slow-moving. Often showers will build up behind retreating cold fronts (or occlusions) and it is therefore as well to say something more about showery situations.

When Showers are Forecast

To make up their minds about the possibility of showers occurring the forecasters look at tephigrams. These are plots of temperature and humidity up through the atmosphere and into the stratosphere. Every day, twice a day, and always simultaneously throughout the world, radiosonde balloons are sent aloft which transmit radio signals indicating pressure, temperature and humidity. In conjunction with the tephigrams the forecasters estimate tomorrow's maximum temperature from a knowledge of how much heat we shall get from the sun. When plotted on the tephigram it is usually easy to see if showers will occur. Showers grow big when the upper air is cold compared to the ground, and if it is relatively humid then they grow frequent as well.

As pointed out under 'Confidence Tricks' only you will be able to recognise exactly when a shower is about to send a big gust and a sudden sheet of cold rain through the fleet, but the order of events is usually much the same.

It is normal to have lowered wind speed (that is, a lull) just before the gust from a shower-cloud strikes (Fig. 7.2). The wind rises sharply and there may be a preliminary gust (a gust tongue) (see page 159) before the true gust edge comes. It is normal for gust and rain to come together unlike a thunderstorm where they may not coincide in time. Unless the shower is part of an air-mass trough (page 23) or in some other way is not individual, the events described for gust cells in Chapter 29 will occur. The wind will veer as the gust strikes, but it is most important to resist tacking on the first heading shift in case it is a short-lived gust tongue. The set of wind shifts associated with one shower cloud may last ten to fifteen minutes or even more and so waiting half a minute before tacking is not going to make that much difference.

The gust wind will blow strong and consistently as the heaviest rain is falling, but will then begin to shift back towards its original direction as the rain starts to ease. In the rear of the passing shower it will become fully backed (shifted anticlockwise) and when the sun comes out again the wind will normally have lulled.

That is how most showers behave unless they are very big and akin to thunderstorms in size and appearance. Sometimes, especially in spring, massive shower clouds grow as the sun gets to the land, but as each needs its

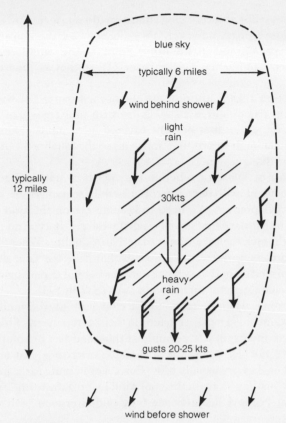

Figure 7.2 *The personal space of a typical shower cloud on a blustery day. Compare the winds under a shower cloud with those under a thunderstorm (Fig. 27.5) – they are not the same*

own personal space in which to build so they form in cells which may be several miles across. Theory shows that when cumulus clouds grow in an airstream where the wind does not shift its direction much with height then the personal space they acquire is twice their depth h.

So Cu clouds that are 5000–6000 feet deep (that is, a mile or so high) will occur in corridors some two miles wide. However, showers are often much deeper than this, maybe twice or three times as deep or more. They travel at speeds which are in excess of the highest speed to be found in the gusts at their leading edges and their personal space gets longer in the direction of the wind as the wind speed goes up. Thus a big cumulonimbus which is 3 miles high will occupy a space that is 6 miles wide and perhaps twice this long. Travelling at 30 knots this shower-space would pass in 24 minutes. However, that includes the blue break between the showers.

So in this case you might expect to get a shower every half an hour or so and sometimes really shower-filled airstreams do produce showers with this frequency. More often however, they do not and the showers become irregular in spacing and in intensity. Some of the variations have been covered under 'Confidence Tricks' (page 21), so they will not be repeated here.

In this section I want to point out the normal pattern of wind changes when a shower passes and as a sailing day with showers will often start off with blue skies, which first become covered in cumulus clouds that only later grow big enough to produce showers, so the 'quality' of the wind will change as the day goes on.

The forecast of 'showers' whether they occur or not, immediately tells you that the wind will develop the gust-lull sequences of wind shifts described in Chapter 29. We need to keep an eye on the kind of day it is going to be so that days that are not 'northwesterly' in type do not become confused with ones that are more 'easterly' in quality. When we label an airstream 'northwesterly' we mean winds that have the same attributes as the clear, cool airstream that typically arrives behind departing depressions and has the characteristic direction of NW (SW in SH).

In the morning, when there are no Cu clouds about, the wind shifts may be rather random or even plain curious in their shift pattern. This is because there is still an inversion left a couple of thousand feet or so up which the thermals have not yet been able to break. Airstreams that are going to produce a lot of showers usually blow Force 4 even quite early and shreds of cloud appear bustling along in the cool wind by breakfast-time. You have to allow for that Force 4 being Force 6 by mid-afternoon with some nasty squalls.

The quantity of cloud that develops first thing is a good indicator of the severity of showers to come because showers will need plenty of moisture. So a sudden build-up of cloud early in the day says that the air is very wet. It will not usually cover the whole sky and soon the clouds will begin to break up into more individual lumps each one of which has a potential gust-lull sequence under it. These are often not yet deep enough to produce showers, but they should be on their way to becoming deep enough by mid-morning. You can usually make up your mind if a growing cloud is likely to get big enough to produce showers as shown in Fig. 7.3. Also fast-growing clouds develop skeins of eyebrow-shaped cloud near their tops and that is a very good sign that the cloud will get big.

When the rain starts it brings down the wind aloft with it so that we suddenly get a gust and a veer with the deluge. The result is a squall. Treat the wind shifts under a shower as if they were just a big gust-cell sequence as outlined in Chapter 30. When beating, starboard tack is given a lift at the head of the shower and later, as it passes, port tack is favoured. The whole thing normally has a duration which is three or four times that of the gust cells found under smaller cumulus clouds.

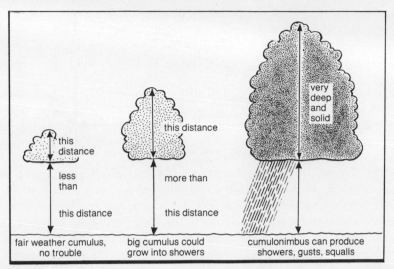

Figure 7.3 *How to get an idea if cumulus clouds are growing big enough to produce showers. If their height off the horizon is more than their depth – no trouble, but if they grow deeper they may be on their way to being shower clouds*

Occasionally cumulonimbus clouds (that is Cu clouds that are big enough to produce precipitation) grow tall enough to develop anvils and then they will command personal spaces maybe 15 miles across and perhaps produce claps of thunder.

A shower cloud will travel roughly with the gradient wind and so may be making 30 knots when the lowest wind speed at the surface is only 10–15 knots. This will increase sharply at the head of the shower to something approaching the gradient speed, say 20–25 knots. The gust will bluster for some minutes and then begin to subside and back in direction (veer in SH) until, as the sun comes out behind the retreating cloud, it is perhaps as much as 30° or more different in direction from the gust. Showers usually start heavy and so do the gusts while they finish with the rain tailing away and at the same time the wind tails away as well.

When you beat through a shower you have to realise that relative to its motion you travel through it at an angle of between 5° and 10° to the windward direction (Fig. 7.4.). This 'apparent course' is explained more fully on page 168, but it comes about because the cloud is travelling towards you at some ten times the speed that you are moving sideways across it.

The apparent course is closer to the true wind direction than the apparent wind because the latter is dictated by the strength of the surface wind which is less than the speed of advance of the shower. Obviously a reach will carry you out through it quicker than any other course. However, when running and overtaken by a shower you will stay with it for longer than you would on dry land. For if you make 10 knots before the wind and the shower travels at

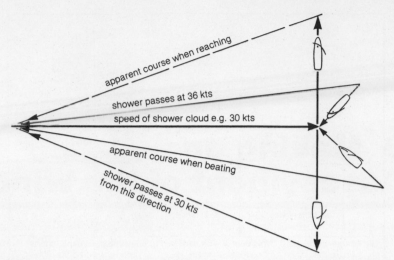

Figure 7.4 *How showers pass on 'apparent courses' when you add their speed to your own*

30 knots in the same direction then the relative speed with which it overhauls you is 20 knots. The higher your downwind performance the longer you spend getting wet but, if you can handle it, you stay in the high-speed wind at the head of the shower for longer and so make more way. Typically you may stay in the worst of the shower for twenty minutes or so.

Showers are big gust cells whose attributes and the tactical reactions to them are gone into in Chapter 29, but for now, when you recognise a shower bearing down on you, note the present wind direction and speed. Expect the direction to veer (shift clockwise) as the rain starts or even just before it starts. At the same time expect the wind speed to double and act accordingly.

As the worst of the bluster subsides expect the wind to shift back towards its direction just before the gusts strikes – and then look out for the next one.

Not all showers will travel at 30 knots. You can assess roughly how fast they are going by guessing the average wind speed and doubling it. However, as the wind is variable in speed you may find it easier to treble the lower wind speed you experience in the blue breaks between the showers.

8 Making an Assessment of the Wind

To get a truly representative idea of what the wind speed and direction will be during the period of a race or a day sail is very difficult. So difficult in fact that most people do not even try to assess it and just take what comes. Sometimes that is all anyone can do, but there are aids to making a more reliable guess at the wind conditions to be found when you break clear of the lee of the clubhouse or the lee of the sheltered channel from which you are sailing.

Firstly, the Beaufort Wind Scale is the framework on which we hang our knowledge of the wind speed. In the following version I have not only included a set of dinghy criteria, but have tried to do the same thing for boards as well. We have to note that the international meteorological brackets of wind speed when plotted on weather maps do not coincide with Beaufort Force. For example, wind arrows on maps fly with the wind and have fleches (or barbs) on them. A full barb means 10 knots ($\pm$ 2 knots) and half a barb 5 knots. Thus a wind arrow with $1\frac{1}{2}$ barbs means that the wind is around 15 knots mean speed, but that is Force 4 on the Beaufort Scale and would, if plotted as such have 2 full barbs as each barb represents 2 Beaufort Forces when plotted that way. Weather maps these days conform to the international scheme and have to be reinterpreted as Beaufort Force. In general if you read wind speed from a weather map then add half a barb to get Beaufort Force, for example a wind around 30 knots is plotted with 3 full barbs, but we would not read that as Force 6 but one up, Force 7.

What will the Wind speed be?

By looking at the charts of wind speed (anemograms) on various pages in Chapters 29 and 30 you will see confirmed something you must already know. The wind is always increasing and decreasing about a mean speed. However, it is the mean speed that will be given to you in forecasts.

So how do you really make up your mind as to what wind speed to expect? To get a reliable and accurate assessment over the period of a race is difficult and often unnecessary because you can only carry one suit of sails and these

The Scale of Wind Speed for Dinghies and Boards

Beaufort number	General description	Limit of mean speed (knots)	Wind symbol	Land signs	Dinghy criteria	Board criteria	State of sea
0	Calm	less than 1	◎	Smoke rises vertically. Leaves do not stir.	Sails will not fill. Racing flag will not respond. Flies and tell-tales may just respond.	Try pumping. If not stand there and hope for some wind.	Sea mirror-smooth. Calm enough to preserve shape of reflections of sails, masts etc.
1	Light air	1–3		Smoke drifts. Wind vanes do not respond.	Sails fill. Racing flags may not be reliable. Flies and tell-tales respond. Crew and helmsman on opposite sides of the craft.	Six square metre sails fill and board begins to make steady speed.	Scaly or shell-shaped ripples No foam crests to be seen on open sea.
2	Light breeze	4–6		Wind felt on face. Leaves rustle. Light flags not extended. Wind vanes respond.	Useful way can be made. Racing flag reliable. Helmsman and crew both sit to windward.	Power developed in sail. Board accelerates smoothly No need to hike out yet.	Small short wavelets with glassy crests that do not break.
3	Gentle breeze	7–10		Light flags extended. Leaves in constant motion.	Helmsman and crew sit on weather gunwale. Spinnakers fill. Fourteen-footers and above may plane.	Easy sailing on all points. Board planing on a reach. Lightweights hike out.	Large wavelets. Crests may break but foam is of glassy appearance. A few scattered white horses may be seen when wind at upper limit.
4	Moderate breeze	11–16		Most flags extend fully. Small branches move. Dust and loose paper may	Dinghy crews lie out. Twelve-foot dinghies may plane: longer dinghies will plane.	Nice conditions. Board now planing on all points but maybe only just downwind	Small waves lengthen. Fairly frequent white horses.

40

Force	Description	Speed		On land	Dinghies	Boards	Sea state
5	Fresh breeze	17–21		Small trees in leaf sway. Tops of tall trees in noticeable motion.	Dinghies ease sheets in gusts. Crews use all weight to keep craft upright. Genoas near their limit. Some capsizes.	Beginners having problems luffing up on conventional boards. Advanced techniques required. Foot straps useful. Very fast sailing.	Moderate waves. Many white horses.
6	Strong breeze	22 to 27		Large branches in motion. Whistling heard in wires.	Dinghies overpowered when carrying full sail. Many capsizes. Crews find difficulty in holding craft upright even when spilling wind.	No room for error. Becoming airborne on waves. Use a 4 square metre sail.	Large waves form and extensive foam crests are prevalent. Spray may be blown off some wave tops
7	Near gale (American usage: Moderate gale)	28–33		Whole trees in motion. Inconvenience felt when walking against wind.	Dinghies fully reefed. Difficult to sail even on main alone. This is the absolute top limit for dinghies – other than in extremis.	Watch the experts.	Sea heaps up and white foam from breaking waves begins to be blown in streaks along the wind direction.
8	Gale (Fresh gale)	34–40		Twigs broken off trees. Generally impedes progress on foot. Rarely experienced inland.	Dinghies may survive if expertly handled in the seaway on foresail alone.	Rescue the experts or have a go at speed record.	Moderately high waves of greater length. Edges of crests begin to break into spindrift. Foam blown in well-marked streaks along the wind.

will be chosen for the conditions you think will obtain through most of the race.

The wind speed is composed of three components:

i the mean wind speed dictated by the local pressure pattern,
ii the gusts and lulls due to up-and-down thermal currents (convection),
iii turbulent eddies and overturnings due to collison of the wind with surface obstacles.

As explained on page 13 the forecast of wind speed comes from making educated guesses as to the distance apart of the isobars on a future weather map or, for immediate use, from an actual map. In either case what the upper and lower wind speeds will be above and below this mean speed is not quoted unless you specifically ask for it. I was talking to an Australian who runs a weather consultancy in Sydney. The mixed professional and amateur crews who sail the over-canvassed Sydney 18–footers in Sydney Harbour are regularly on the phone to him wanting to know the wind speed to within a few knots by the end of the afternoon or whenever so that they can bend on the correct weight of canvas. For most dinghy classes the matter of sail weight is academic as they are only allowed one weight anyway, but as a Firefly sailor – about the most restricted of any dinghy class – I never found this a disadvantage. Quite the reverse as you did not have to curse yourself afterwards for choosing the wrong suit. Board sailors will be in the same boat (to coin a phrase) and while I read of someone during a high-powered Hawaiian meeting changing boards half way round, that again is not likely to be more than a chance event.

The important wind speed is going to be the strongest you are likely to experience and something can be said about that. Firstly there is a principle to be remembered:

Unstable (heap-cloud) days produce the biggest variation in wind speed.
Stable (layer-cloud) days produce less variation.

It is the unstable days on which we must particularly concentrate and remember that the bigger the individual heap clouds the bigger the gusts to be expected. Thus skies with *cumulus* will produce the smallest speed variations in the spectrum while those with *cumulonimbus* will produce intermediate variations and when big cumulonimbus clouds come along then the gusts can sometimes quadruple the speed.

With this in mind we give a useful table which will enable you to read off the likely and maximum gust speeds with given actual or forecast mean speeds.

It is important to realise that as gusts are wind coming down from above the shoreside shelter may not be effective in reducing their speed. Thus a gusty day may find normally sheltered waters with a very wide divergence between the wind that blows for most of the time and that which comes along in the gusts.

Forecast mean speed	Average gust speed	Maximum gust speed
Force 4 (10–16 knots)	5–6	6–7
Force 5 (16–21 knots)	6–7	8
Force 6 (21–27 knots)	8	9 (gale warnings for sea areas when gusts get this strong)
Force 7 (27–33 knots)	8–9	10
Force 8 (33–40 knots)	9–10	10

Morning periods will produce the highest variation between gusts and lulls whereas afternoon conditions, when the mean speed goes up to its maximum, will not appear to have the same variability. The gust speed will be much the same as the morning or a little higher, but the lower mean speed of the morning thus makes the gusts seem stronger.

Making a Wind Speed Assessment

You can ask a local and representative weather office what their wind speed is and what the gusts are going to be, but remember that they will probably have an anemometer head that is way up and therefore may be over-estimating your situation. However, as water surfaces are so smooth if you have a good fetch in the wind direction they may be under-estimating the speed. Even so the gusts they have and those you will have will be much the same – until big showers or thunderstorms come along.

If the club has an anemometer then that will give a pretty reliable estimate unless you are due to be towed out for an Olympic-style triangle off the coast in which case put up the speed by a Beaufort force or so. Again the gust speed will not be much different ashore or afloat – only the mean speed will up a Beaufort force.

If you have to assess it on the spot with no aids then make sure you get out, somewhere clear and elevated, say on the sea wall facing the wind or somewhere where the shore-hamper is not going to give a low value. If river sailing it may be impossible to get a reliable assessment and you will have to take it as it comes. However, allow for the 'down escalator' that brings gusts into even quite enclosed tree-canyons leaving you with alternate periods of no wind and sudden puffs that may take you to where there is even less wind.

At inland sites generally the mean wind speed is controlled by the land over which the wind comes and you need to be out in the open to get the right assessment of speed. However, allow, as in Chapter 23, for what the shore-cover does to the wind in its lee.

Making a Wind Direction Assessment

You will find from the evidence of Chapter 31 that sometimes the wind's repeating pattern may have a period of as much as ten minutes or more and with easterly winds it may be up to fifteen or twenty minutes. Thus unless you are prepared to study the wind direction variations before a race for what may seem a long time, you may be surprised to find that the wind on the water is nothing like the one you observed before setting sail.

The principle established at the outset of this section will apply here. If conditions are stable (there are layer clouds or it is early morning or evening etc.) then the wind you observe is probably the wind you will have. However, allow for the 'wind's day' (page 116) and if it is unstable then try to allow some time to relax, lie on your back and watch the way the flags on the clubhouse shift in direction or the racing flags of dinghies in the park. Very warm mornings with islands of altocumulus clouds dotted about the sky may have very abnormal shift patterns that take a long while to assess.

When you have a good idea of the extreme directions to which the wind is on average veering and backing (and you may have to ignore some very extreme values) then take the intermediate direction between these and that is the mean direction. As pointed out on page 172 it is helpful to locate a topographic feature miles away near the eye of the mean wind in order to have a reference for wind shifts when you are trying to use them tactically.

9 For How Long will the Wind Shift?

There will be a great deal said about wind shifts in this book because in the end it is winds that shift for you or against you at crucial moments in races that make the difference between win or lose. So before we get down to details of whys and wherefores let us divide up the wind shifts by the time there is between one shift and the next.

There are, for us, permanent wind shifts where the wind changes direction and stays that way for periods of more than a day. There are semi-permanent windshifts that can alter the wind during say a race or a day's meeting after which the wind stays more-or-less in its new direction. Finally there are micro windshifts whose time period we can measure in minutes (Fig. 9.2).

The permanent shifts very often come when depressions are approaching or receding and they may be a gradual change from one direction to another that occupies some hours. Typical examples include Fig. 9.1.

Figure 9.1 *Wind shifts of a run of changeable weather with typical times between the various features*

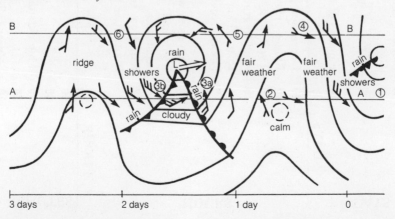

DAYS	
20	blocking anticyclones persist up to 20 weeks
10	Periods of high pressure — Cyclonic periods when lows become quasi-stationary
2 DAYS	Families of depressions
HOURS	
40	Depression pass
30	Ridges between depressions pass
20	Typical time for — Wind sometimes blows from same direction
10	wind to grow from
8	15 to 25 kts when low approaches — Small local low pass
6	Rain from warm fronts and — Seabreezes last this long
4	occlusions
2	Rain from cold fronts — Phases of mountain and valley winds
	Heat lows over land
MINUTES	
60	1 HOUR
50	
40	
30	Thunderstorms pass — Shifts due to older fronts and occlusions
20	
10	Shower cells pass — Shift phases in 'easterlies'

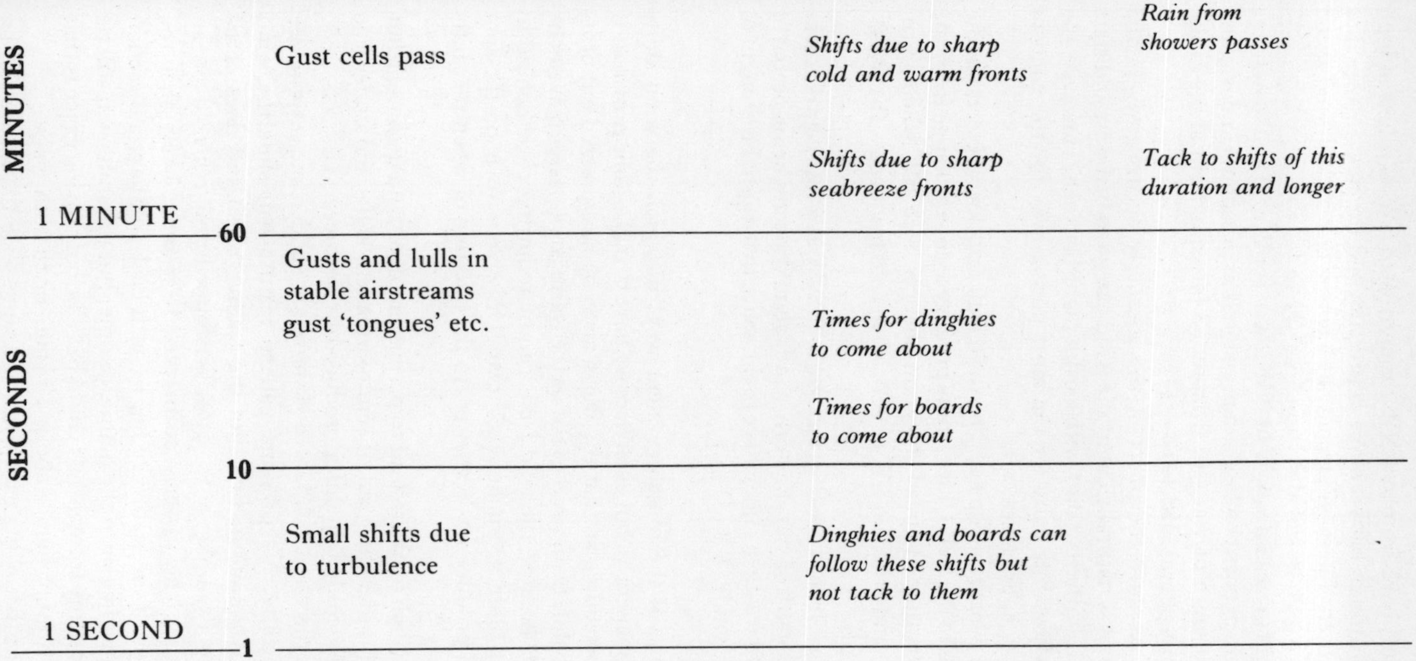

Figure 9.2 *The time spectrum of wind changes*

1 Winds that shift back from say NW through W to SW as ridges of high pressure run through between one depression and the next in a spell of unsettled weather. There will usually be a period of very low wind speed between the two phases of direction. AA ① → ②

2 A slow shift and increase from W or NW towards SW or S and sometimes as far as SE which occurs when a depression is approaching and is going to track to the south of you (see Chapter 33 for equivalent shifts in the Southern Hemisphere). BB ④ → ⑤

Sometimes because the onset of the southerly occurs early in the morning when it is naturally calm, the wind can go to bed west and start the day from a southerly point with a calm night between. However, the more-or-less slow shift is by far the most normal way for the wind to change as a low approaches.

3 Sudden shifts when fronts pass. The wind shifts clockwise (veers) in the NH, but backs in the SH. Older fronts produce a slower change from one direction to another. Typical direction changes S to SW when warm fronts pass (a) and are from SW to NW when cold fronts pass (b) (NH). AA ③ⓐ and ③ⓑ

4 Winds that back from E or SE through N to NW as a low centre tracks through to the south of you. Easterly winds should always be suspected of harbouring bad weather somewhere to the south that might be brought to you on upper winds. BB ⑤ → ⑥

These are some of the most prevalent ways in which the wind shifts more-or-less permanently, but even here we have to make some provisos. If a depression is occluding so that the warm air is being squeezed out of its warm sector, the shift from say S to SW as the warm front passes may not be at all permanent, because the cold front can be following close behind to produce another shift in an hour or two. Only your own on-the-spot observations can produce ready answers to the question of when the shifts are likely.

Such events, which ought to lead to permanent new wind directions but do not, must fall under the head of semi-permanent shifts and under this head we have to include the shifts produced by seabreezes.

Charts of wind direction in Chapter 31 show how sudden and extreme are seabreeze wind shifts. No pressure-pattern feature will shift the wind through 180° in a minute or two, but the seabreeze can and does. This occurs when, for example, a W wind is stopped and reversed on an east-facing coast by the easterly seabreeze. It is more likely that the off-shore wind which the seabreeze has to push back will have a direction which is not perpendicular to the main coastline, but the shifts will still be greater than almost any frontal shift could be. The only saving grace is that the wind speeds are not high – about 10 knots or so both ways.

Another system that shifts the wind on a time scale that could not be considered permanent is the big thunderstorm. Storms take over the local wind system and impose their own regime on it. They draw in air from round about to feed their updraughts. On a sultry day, especially if you are sailing inland and an unannounced wind springs up, suspect that it is feeding storms that you may not even be aware of. You are, however, more likely to be overtaken by the cold wind that blows from storms and pours out across the countryside like cold water.

In this bracket we must also include mountain and valley winds of highland regions plus simpler katabatic winds that tend to blow in the evenings off the higher ground plus anabatics that tend to blow by day towards the high ground. Both katabatics and anabatics need sun or clear skies to make an appearance and as they tend normally to be weak they also thrive in anticyclonic or other conditions when little gradient wind exists.

Finally we must introduce the micro-changes that are induced in airstreams mainly through the agency of thermals. Whenever land is heated by the sun it becomes a potential source of thermals and these rising currents and the compensating down currents that surround them introduce variability into wind speed and direction. Thermals lead to the gust and lull patterns experienced in variable winds as well as sometimes producing the only wind in flat-calm conditions. The former of these is covered in Chapter 29 and the latter in Chapter 22.

The smallest-scale shifts in the wind are of the order of a few seconds in duration and are due to turbulent overturnings and eddies induced by surface obstacles. They are a menace to small-boat sailors as they tend to mask the real wind shifts that can have tactical advantages.

How all these features and others mentioned in the rest of the book tie up on the time scale from a few seconds to a few months is shown in Fig. 9.2.

10 The Wind's Day

You do not have to sail a dinghy or board for very long to realise that sometimes the wind is pretty steady and at other times very variable. With more experience you find that the steady periods coincide very often with evening and early morning, while the variable times come along most often during the morning and afternoon.

This can be understood when we appreciate the idea of stability and instability of the air deck next to the surface. We will call this the 'sailing layer' and note that very often the atmosphere is layered like a multi-decker sandwich so that the sailing layer is just the lowest of a set of air decks with different characteristics right up to the top of the atmosphere (Fig. 10.1).

We are concerned with the first two (or perhaps three) such layers because what happens in the air decks immediately above the surface layer has a strong bearing on the sailing wind. This follows from the way air moves between layers of different temperatures. If a warm air deck lies over a cool one the warm air tends to sink onto the cool and as air is trying to settle towards the surface this inhibits upward convection currents and the air is 'stable'. Stable situations tend to produce steady winds as well as damping down wind speed. Calms by day almost invariably mean a very stable layer near the ground with warm air not far above the ground.

Conversely, if a cool layer overlies a warmer one, bubbles of warm air rise into and through the cool layer. This is an unstable situation and as what goes up must come down, so compensating cool air currents sink towards the surface. We see that an unstable situation tends to mix up the air decks, while a stable one tends to separate them and keep them distinctly different.

There is a simple principle which helps sort this out. The principle (which is universal in nature) is:

Heat seeks cold.

Looking at Fig. 10.1 which summarises what has just been said, notice in the stable situation (b) that warm air layers sink onto cool ones. In the unstable situation (a) the warm air rises into the cool and both obey the 'Heat seeks cold' principle. Put a poker in a fire and heat flows from the hot

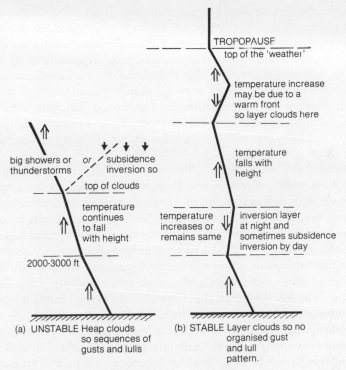

Figure 10.1 *The way the temperature drops off with height on (a) unstable days and (b) stable days. Decks of layered clouds exist where inversion or isothermal (no change in temperature with height) layers exist*

end to the cold end, which is the same principle. You can solve a great number of meteorological puzzles with this simple idea.

The normal situation during the day when most sailing is done is (a), because the earth's surface warms up with the day and communicates its heat to the surface layer. Thermal bubbles push off upwards from near the ground to seek cooler air above and cooler sinking currents come down around them. Note that this applies to small waters where the wind is blowing off the land, or to coastwise waters with wind blowing from a landmass. The sea does not change temperature with the day although changes do occur due to warmed or cooled tidal streams from estuaries and creeks (see page 92).

In the late afternoon of a normal sunny or fair day the instability of the day is first neutralised and then reverses into stability. This is easily understood because the land is cooling as the sun sinks lower in the sky and the sailing layer now cools in sympathy. However, the thermals have warmed the air above and the situation shown in (b) obtains. The sailing layer becomes more and more stable as this process goes on and stability

51

means that the surface wind becomes separated from the wind above it and cannot get any help from the latter in keeping up its speed. So gradually it loses its momentum as it collides with surface obstacles and the result is the well-known one where the wind goes down with the evening. The process strengthens during the night so that even when there is a moderate wind by day the period around dawn may be almost calm. Given a sheltered harbour, creek or reservoir the number of mornings with calms may be very substantial and there are some places especially in more sub-tropic climes where in summer there may be more than an even chance that the morning will be calm.

It is under this stable situation that you may well set sail in the morning and so there will be very little wind, the water will be almost mirror calm and it will seem that any racing to come will be a set of drifting matches. However, as soon as the sun gets onto the land – and even if there is no direct sun so long as the temperature rises – the trend to instability will start.

The change from one air deck to another with different characteristics is not normally abrupt. It is very like having a sandwich with say two slices of white bread (the cool layers) and a slice of filling (the warm layer in between). The filling is where the characteristics change and in the case of a stable situation (b) it is called an 'inversion' layer.

It is normal to have inversions over the land at night, but they can exist in many other situations and at all kinds of levels. In fact wherever clouds stop growing there must be some kind of inversion. To be exact we have to include isothermal layers here, but as they produce the same effect so we will call all such layers inversions. When fleets of cumulus clouds grow over the sea and there is no obvious land influence, their tops are usually cut off at about all one level. So at that level there is an inversion. It may be several thousands of feet up while the overnight inversion is usually only one to two thousand feet up, if that, but the effect is the same. Inversions put lids on the layers below them and stop the clouds growing through them until such times as the lower layer gets so heated as to enable its thermals to punch holes in the inversion above it.

This is of course what happens to the overnight inversion as the sun climbs higher in the sky and as soon as the wind begins to pick up you know that the inversion is breaking down. It does not do so all at once, but in sections so that at first the wind may be fitful. However, once the process has started you can expect the inversion to go and the wind to grow and become much more reliable.

The practical reason for knowing about how inversions form and break is that it helps understand how the wind at the surface can decrease or increase without any change appearing in the weather map. Almost everybody is aware that when the isobaric 'tramlines' on the weather map get closer together the wind has to increase as well and of course the converse also applies. Yet in settled anticyclonic weather, when there may seem to be no appreciable change in the isobaric pattern around the 'High', the wind increases by day and decreases by night so that under the same isobars it can be calm at breakfast-time and perhaps 10–15 knots or more after lunch.

The way the wind usually changes through the twenty-four hours is shown in Fig. 10.2 and this cyclic pattern is called the 'diurnal' (or daily) variation. It all comes about because of the way the temperature rises and the thermals thrust up to higher levels by day and because inversions form by night. What happens is that breaking an inversion taps the wind that was locked away above it so that chunks of it appear in the previously sluggish surface wind and so speed up the latter. As wind speed tends to increase with height, so when in the afternoon thermals reach high, they bring down the strongest wind of the day. As the sun sinks thermals become inhibited and the exchange of wind between surface and above is curtailed and eventually ceases altogether.

This idea of exchanging fast wind speed above with slower wind speed from below through the agency of thermals is very important if you are to understand and make use of the way sailing winds are constructed, so that you can get real tactical advantage from the micro wind shifts in the

Figure 10.2 *The diurnal (daily) change of air temperature and the corresponding changes in wind speed and cloudiness*

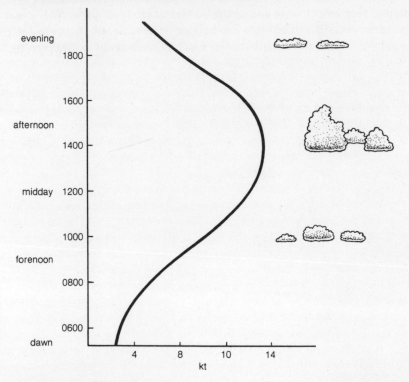

airstreams that come your way. For example the above ideas tell us that the wind is likely to be most variable when the inversion is breaking down in the early forenoon of a fair day, but that later it will settle down to a shift pattern that is in some ways predictable. We will not expect this shift pattern to survive after about five in the afternoon when the inversion is forming and evening sailing will have steady periods of wind, but the well-known 'holes' will appear in it as time goes on until long before summer sundown it may be gone almost entirely. The evening calm is likely to come down quite early and last through the evening after a day when a seabreeze has set in against a light off-shore wind. Here the opposition of seabreeze and land wind aids the inversion in reducing the coastal area to breathlessness. There often will not be any more wind until after nightfall when the nocturnal wind begins to blow from the land to the sea, but that is rather academic for dinghies and boards unless you engage in moonlight sailing matches.

In these ways (and for the reasons given) the wind goes through its daily cycle which is most evident with winds that are around moderate strength, but even with strong to gale-force winds is still there so that the mid-afternoon sees the strongest blow of the day and the wind moderates with evening. Both temperature and cloudiness follow the same variation, but we have seen that thermals grow as the temperature increases which explains why the two grow and wane together. Cumulus clouds are a visible sign of thermals at work and as the growth of these clouds is such a useful pointer to things that are about to happen or have already happened to the wind we go into their attributes in much greater detail in Chapter 29.

11 Wind and Pressure

With a few exceptions weather travels from west to east, and that goes for both hemispheres. The depressions that cross South Africa and South Australia are just as much pushed along by the upper westerlies as those that cross the North Atlantic and North Pacific Oceans. Only the direction in which the winds rotate about the lows and highs differs in the two hemispheres.

In the Northern Hemisphere the winds rotate clockwise round good weather systems (highs) and anticlockwise round the bad weather systems (lows). In the Southern Hemisphere it is exactly the opposite with the winds moving about the low centres clockwise and anticlockwise about the highs (Fig. 2.1).

The large-scale winds of the world are always trying to blow from where pressure is high to where it is low. Near the equator they manage this in more-or-less the way you would expect, that is, wind blows directly from regions on the weather map marked 'High' to those marked 'Low'. In the temperate latitudes (where most of the readers of this book will sail) another effect appears due to the rotation of the Earth. This effect increases as the sine of the latitude and so at the equator, where the latitude is zero, the effect is also zero, but at 50°N (or S) it rises to become three-quarters of its highest value, whch is found at the poles.

The effect is called the geostrophic effect and, without going into unnecessary detail, it looks to Earth-bound mortals as if the air is constantly being diverted to the right of its path. The end result (as shown in Fig. 11.1) is that the wind ends up blowing between the centres of low and high pressure, rather than directly from one to another. This relationship between wind direction and pressure distribution in any locality can be summed up in some simple practical rules:

(NH) Stand BACK to the wind and pressure is LOW on your LEFT hand.
(SH) Stand FACING the wind and pressure is LOW on your LEFT hand.

The above tells the practical dinghy or board sailor all he needs to know about the relationship between wind direction and the local pressure pattern. If you sail near the equator, you must remember that local wind

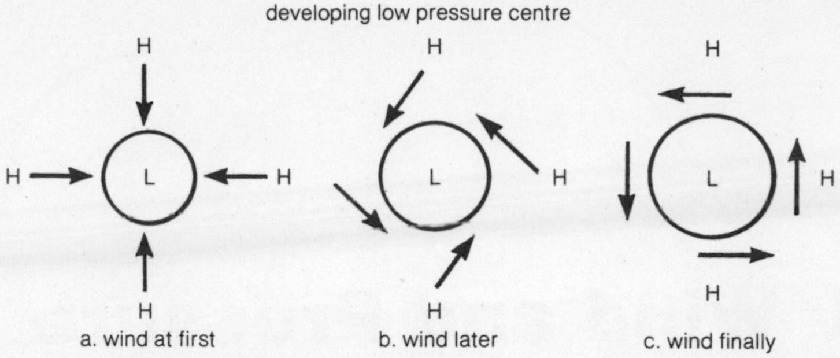

H ↓   H ↓   H

H → (L) ← H   (L) H   (L) H

H ↑   H ↑   H

a. wind at first   b. wind later   c. wind finally

Figure 11.1 *The way the earth's rotation acts on wind that blows from where pressure is higher (H) to where it is lower (L)*

effects are going to become increasingly important and will often override local pressure gradients. This also applies in light winds in temperate latitudes where winds due to differential heating of land and water often take over and produce surface winds that bear no relation to the existing pressure pattern.

The most important of these is the seabreeze as this may affect almost any coastal belt and seabreezes can penetrate many tens of miles inland under favourable circumstances. The night-time equivalent, the land breeze, need not be referred to since dinghy and board sailing is a daylight practice.

Local heat depressions may form well inland on hot days and induce winds to blow into them from their surroundings. They often nurture heavy thunderstorms. Otherwise local hill or mountain slopes that see the sun will have rising air currents on them and anabatic winds result (page 151). Conversely, previously sunlit slopes become shadowed with the day and as a result sinking air will induce katabatic winds (page 151). The combination of these effects lead to mountain and valley winds that often affect high lakes and reservoirs (page 149). These and other local wind effects only really come into their own when the pressure pattern is slack and winds are light, that is, Force 3 or less.

Which introduces us to wind speed. Wind that blows to keep low pressure on its left (NH) tends to be thrown to the right of its path more strongly as the wind speed increases. So, as the opposing force is the pressure gradient force (P.G.), the amount the pressure falls with distance between high and low must be greater there than elsewhere. This is shown at (A) in Fig. 11.2. It is like having two springs in tension. One, the pressure gradient 'spring' (P.G.) pulls the wind arrow towards low pressure. The other, the geostrophic force 'spring' (G.F.) pulls the wind arrow towards high pressure. Normally the two tensions are the same and the gradient wind, in the direction of neither, sails along between them thereby losing no energy.

We see from the above that wherever the wind is stronger the lines of equal pressure (isobars) must be closer together. As the isobars are for

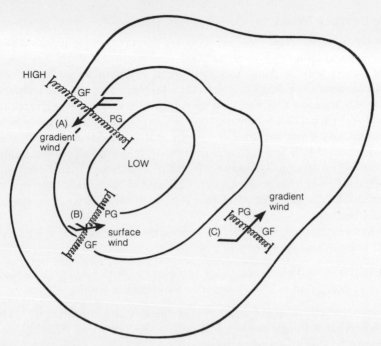

Figure 11.2 *Where the spacing of the isobars is tight (A) the balance between geostrophic force (G.F.) and pressure gradient force (P.G.) is represented by two tightly stretched springs. The gradient wind blows along the isobars between these two opposing forces. Where the spacing is open (C) the springs are less tightly stretched. The surface wind (B) is deflected towards low pressure by the P.G. force remaining the same, but the G.F. force declines as surface wind speed declines*

pressure as contours are for height, so by analogy the rapidity with which the pressure falls with distance is called the 'gradient' of the isobars. Very close isobars, like very close contours, indicate a steep gradient, but from the balance between gradient force and geostrophic force outlined above, the wind speed must be high there to keep the balance between the two forces. A more detailed explanation can be found in my book *Cruising Weather* which is a companion volume to this.

Here I am thinking of the practical dinghy or board sailors who are not really interested in the deep theory behind wind effects, but are obviously keen to know those results that affect them and their performance around the buoys. There are good books which give the mathematical basis of wind effects useful to sailors, but these have no place in this book (see bibliography).

The Surface Wind

In the previous section we have looked at the way the gradient wind blows about lows and highs. This is the large-scale wind under whose influence most sailing will be done. Certainly fresh winds of Force 5 and some moderate winds of Force 4 will override local thermal winds like seabreezes and mountain and valley winds. With lighter winds we can never be entirely sure that the wind that is blowing has not been modified in some way by the surroundings. Even the stronger winds will be affected by the terrain, blowing round hills and mountains, funnelling down valleys and fanning out onto open stretches of water. Shoreside effects will divert even quite strong winds when the conditions are right and so the surface wind may not be at all like the gradient wind that the isobars on the weather map say should be there.

Whatever the terrain the surface wind is never the same as the gradient wind anyway and varies in two ways:

  i the surface wind blows at an angle across the isobars out of high into low,
 ii the surface wind is less strong than the gradient wind.

Both these effects are of importance to dinghy and board sailors as they will affect such things as choice of sails, choice of crew, what optimum course to take on the next mark etc.

To understand why the surface wind blows at an angle across the isobars, go back to the spring analogy of the last section. We envisaged the gradient wind arrow being the victim of a tug of war between the pressure gradient force (P.G.) and the geostrophic force (G.F.), but of the two only the latter depends on the wind speed while the former will not change if the wind speed drops.

Obstacles in the way of the wind will naturally make it slow down so that while the P.G. spring stays at the same tension, the G.F. spring weakens. This allows the P.G. force to haul the wind across the isobars from the high side to the low side. In this way air that starts off blowing out of high pressure centres ends up blowing into low pressure ones ((B) in Fig 11.2a).

It must be realised from this that the gradient wind is the wind that blows way above our mast tops unimpeded by surface friction and that the surface wind is backed to its direction (shifted anticlockwise) in the Northern Hemisphere and veered (shifted clockwise) in the Southern.

It also follows that the more the surface slows the wind the greater the angle between gradient and surface winds. It is usually assumed that we are clear of surface friction when we get above about 2000 feet (600 metres), but this is a rough rule that we say more about on page 36. Sometimes the surface wind layer is only a few hundred feet deep and at other times it may reach up as high as 4000–5000 feet. It all depends on the weather conditions.

The rough rule for the degree by which the gradient and surface winds differ in direction and speed is as follows:

Over the open sea: 15° difference in direction.
                       Surface wind = $\frac{1}{3}$ gradient speed.

Over the land: 30° difference in direction.
                       Surface wind = $\frac{2}{3}$ gradient speed.

These facts are summed up in Fig. 4.1.

We shall see the practical results of this knowledge on page 183, but for now suffice to say that the stronger puffs in an airstream are chunks of gradient wind brought down from above into the surface wind and so the faster and slower parts of an airstream have different directions – an important point when maximum way is to be made.

12 The Shape
of Depressions

When you look at a weather map, to a first approximation depressions are round. There are going to be all kinds of variations on this basically round shape, but if we think of isobars being circles round a low centre we can more easily envisage the wind changes that will come along as the centre tracks past.

Ahead of a travelling depression there are three main zones where you may be sailing and which will experience a different set of wind shifts. These are illustrated in Fig. 12.1a. If you are south of where the centre will track the wind will back at first and then veer. Backing means an anticlockwise shift and veering a clockwise shift, and the changes described refer to the Northern Hemisphere. For the Southern Hemisphere interchange back for veer and veer for back wherever they occur (Fig. 12.1b).

There will normally be some form of ridge of high pressure both ahead and behind a travelling low and, allowing for the fact that the surface wind blows out across the isobars from high presure and into low, the wind in the ridge twenty-four hours or so ahead of the arrival of the low centre will be W or SW. Here are some pointers to a coming depression which can include:

i the forecast that warns of a low moving in to affect your area,
ii the sight of a high cirrus (mares' tails) cloud moving in above any other cloud there may be,
iii the backing of the wind into the southern quadrants even though there is not much sign of any other change,
iv a falling barometer. The latter is not going to be greatly stressed here as dinghy and board sailors do not carry barometers although they may be able to see one in the clubhouse.

To simplify the text the following descriptions of wind directions and shifts etc. are going to be for the NH. Readers in the SH will be able to deduce the changes to be made from the last example (Fig. 12.1b).

Pointer (iii) above only applies when the depression centre is going to track to the north of your position and when the centre tracks to the south the wind in the ridge will usually go through a calm period before picking up from E or around there. There will be high cloud moving in here also, but it may not appear as soon as it will when you are south of the centre or on the depressions track.

Thus if you are expecting a low to be coming in and the wind goes east and tends to stay there, you can expect the wind shifts that go with the passage of a depression centre to the south of you. From Fig. 12.1a we see that these shifts will be a more-or-less gradual backing in direction until the centre has moved on when it may well be N. It is usually the case that the wind strength will not be great, but low cloud, murk and drizzle or continuous rain are to be expected within a couple of hundred miles of the centre. Further out it may just be cloudy or it can even be that you will be in the sunshine while to the south you can see the cloud-mass of the depression going by.

When you are on the direct path of the low the wind will be somewhere around SE at first and it can increase to fresh or more before it sinks in speed again. If the centre passes over you then it will be a case of sitting, maybe stemming the tide as you strive for the next mark, with the rain trickling

Figure 12.1 *The wind shifts to expect when in three different positions relative to a coming low pressure centre (a) for the northern hemisphere (b) for the southern hemisphere*

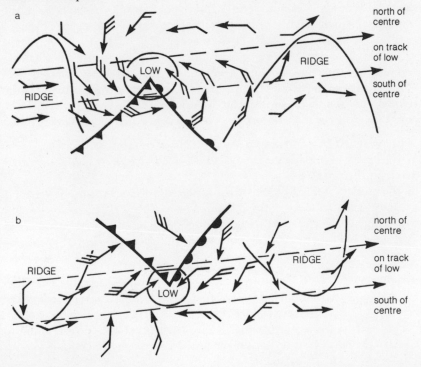

down your neck and with hardly any wind. All you can do is wait until the centre passes (akin to the 'eye' of a hurricane but somewhat less hairy) and the wind comes in from some westerly point and then strengthens with time to eventually break into clearing skies and with a NW cant to it.

These latter shifts may not be quite as depicted as it depends entirely which side of the exact depression centre you happen to be. The complex shifts are described in the shipping forecasts as 'cyclonic' and that term indicates a depression will track through the area without anyone knowing quite where it will go, thus leaving it up to the mariner on the spot to make up his own mind. Even so, by knowing the shape of the depression and its wind structure you can often say where you are with respect to the centre.

13 Depressions and How They are Made

In our quest for the important facts about weather that are of practical help to dinghy and board sailors, it is very useful to be able to anticipate coming changes of wind direction based on what the weather has been and what it is now.

We have to face it that there are going to be many occasions when the wind will take a new set without any reliable sign of the impending change, but there are sky and other signs connected with the advancing, passing and departing depression that will help in making fairly immediate tactical decisions and also aid the more strategic plans you make when you are thinking out how to sail a race which is coming up either later in the day or tomorrow.

The depressions of temperate latitudes are like eddies in a circumpolar river of westerly winds. They derive their energy from the difference in temperature between their warm and cold parts and a strong contrast between the cold air to the north and the warm air to the south of a depression centre makes for a vigorous depression.

In the North Atlantic area the two air masses that create the depressions are both comparatively wet and are thus labelled 'maritime'. The cold one comes south from polar waters and so becomes a 'maritime Polar' air mass (mP). The warm one comes from the large semi-permanent anticyclone over sub-tropical seas between the Azores and America and is therefore labelled 'maritime Tropical' (mT).

These two air masses have entirely different weather and wind characteristics. The polar air mass is always finding itself over warmer water or land and so it becomes showery. Its attributes are from a visual point of view those of a *cumulonimbus*, and the airstream is variable in speed and direction. Big gusts and squalls accompany virile outbreaks of mP air and many capsizes result as crews fail to meet the challenge of the gusts. Showers are the trade-mark of the mP air and we find it at its best (or worst) just after a depression has passed and the wind has shifted to somewhere around northwest. Visibility will be good and the whole air mass has a well-washed look with cool days and quite cold nights under stars that shine like jewels in the crisp air.

The maritime Tropical air mass could not be more different from the maritime Polar air mass. The most likely wind direction for this air mass is southwest and it is often muggy-warm at any time of year. The cloud that accompanies it is quite unlike the mP air, being prone to layers of low, dark lumpy stratus cloud. When the low cloud does clear it is often only temporary and your impression of the upper sky is of one of many layers of cloud at different heights. This is the air mass that brings fog both to the sea coasts and certainly to the higher ground inland. Sailing a high lake or reservoir with a typically Force 4 maritime Tropical airstream can lead to real problems finding your way from one mark to the next and the conditions can go on being murky literally for days when the wind sticks in the SW quarter.

Here is a summary of the major attributes of these two air masses plus a few more.

Abbreviation	Name	Typical Weather
mT	maritime Tropical	Extensively cloudy with rain and drizzle. Poor visibility and fog. Otherwise high humidity and when less cloudy can be very warm for the time of year.
mP	maritime Polar	Full of heap clouds, showers and bright periods. Visibility usually very good. Cool and clear.

While they may have slightly different names in different parts of the world, these two air masses will be found clashing together and spawning strings of depressions. These are the 'wet' air masses and there are others which are much dryer as they come from the centres of great land masses. In Europe they are

cP	continental Polar	Dry, often clear weather. Warm in summer, but can be intensely cold in winter as well as cloudy.
cT	continental Tropical	Dry and very warm for the time of year. Again, often cloudless. In Europe this air mass comes from North Africa very often.

Meteorologists recognise many more air masses than these, but in many parts of the world there are often four such air masses which make the bulk of the airstreams experienced. In Britain the nicest air mass of them all is

| rmP | returning maritime Polar | Full of fair-weather cumulus. Slightly cool but invigorating. Wind usually W but does not breed showers. Visibility good. 'When the wind is in the west then the weather's at its best.' |

It is perhaps useful to point out that these are the attributes of air masses at their most potent. All shades of change can be found in older versions of them. When they come straight out of their source regions they are wet or dry through their whole depth and comparatively cold or warm through their whole depth as well. As time goes on the ground or water over which they travel will modify their lower layers and as these are the layers in which we sail so an mT air mass, for example, may not look much like the outline given above because it has dried out or in some other way been modified. Except by asking a weather office or recognising the conditions for yourself it may sometimes be difficult to make up your mind what kind of air mass you are in. For example, as I write the wind is south – an mT direction but the big drops of heavy showers are beating against the windows – an mP attribute. It is unusual to have showers from a 'warm' quarter, and this odd situation comes about because there is a depression closely to the west and the air is coming round it. In this way an airstream with showery polar attributes can come in from the south simply because a local depression is bringing northerly air round and feeding it to us from another direction.

Another important way in which an air mass changes its attributes is by being eroded from the top by sinking air from very high up. Everyone expects air that goes up to get cooler and to form cloud and rain, but the reverse is also true. Air that sinks get warmer and as warm air can hold more water vapour than cold air so sinking, warming air leads to upper clouds being evaporated away. This process is called subsidence and subsidence is the natural situation in anticyclones and ridges of high pressure.

An anticyclone will have very little cloud at altitude, but it can be cloudy near the ground so that the idea of anticyclonic weather being cloud-free is not always realised. When you are earth-bound it makes little difference if a layer of low cloud has more cloud above it or no cloud above it, it is still cloudy. There is however one difference. In the summer half of the year when the sun has considerable power a cloud layer near the ground will usually be burned off by the heat of the day whereas in the winter half it usually persists. This is one of the major differences between winter and summer weather. Cloud layers near the ground persist in winter even in anticyclones (in fact especially in anticyclones) while such layers often disappear in summer. In similar situations the upper sky will not be much different winter or summer.

As already pointed out there are many other air masses recognised around the world by meteorologists, but wherever you are the wet-warm and wet-cold air masses are the ones which will lead to the formation of depressions. On any day there will be a snakey line of division between the realm of the polar air and the realm of the tropical air encircling the temperate latitudes of the two hemispheres. These more-or-less continuous divisions are called the Polar Fronts. If we describe the North Atlantic Polar Front situation it will, with slight modifications apply equally to the Pacific, or to the Southern Ocean (see Fig. 2.2).

Along the Polar Front mT and mP air masses meet and do battle. Where they meet, the less dense tropical air begins to take on a slope over the polar air while the latter, denser air slides in under the warm air. The result is that a front develops like a wedge between them. However, at the same time the front itself may develop a kink or wave in it. At the tip of the wave, the surface pressure falls and air moves in from the surroundings to try and fill the mini-depression that is forming. At first it blows directly into the tip of the wave but then the geostrophic effect (page 55) acts on it and it ends up blowing round the developing low centre (Fig. 13.1a).

The wave does not stay where it first formed, but begins to run eastwards along the Polar Front. Sometimes it does not develop and simply runs swiftly along the front occasionally at speeds approaching 60 knots entrained by the upper westerlies above it. At other times, and usually when there are no lows already existing near it, the wave develops and the central pressure falls rapidly so engaging more and more air from its surroundings. Now it does not travel so fast, because it is using its energy to deepen and develop.

After a day or two a typical depression is in being which has the main weather regions illustrated in Fig. 13.1b. It is depressions like this that are to be found going through their life cycles along the Polar Fronts of either hemisphere. In Britain and over the Atlantic coastline of Europe depressions that pass are usually fully formed or even past their prime and the normal track is towards Scandinavia where many of them fill up (Fig. 13.1c).

Having said this we must recognise that there is nowhere that may not see one side or another of a depression. They can track to the south of you or to the north and the wind shifts that result in these two typical cases were outlined in the previous chapter. The major problem is not that the wind will shift, but when it will shift. It is the timing of met. events that is always the biggest headache and it is here that the crew on the spot must learn to recognise sky signs of impending change so that they can make up their own minds as to what will happen and when.

Sometimes depressions move round the edges of large anticyclones on odd tracks. They may even on occasions move against the general run of the westerlies and so come in from the east and they are quite easily diverted to move up waterways that lie roughly in their direction of motion. A typical example of this is the 'Channel' depression that prefers to move along the

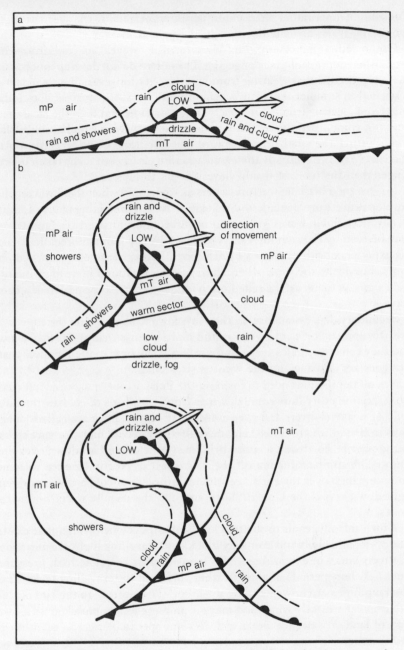

Figure 13.1 *Three stages in the development of a depression (a) a wave low which will sometimes develop into (b) a depression in its prime. The depression will deepen until it begins to occlude as it has done in (c). Then it begins to fill up, but occasionally another low forms on the point of occlusion where the warm and cold fronts meet*

English Channel rather than continue on an original track over the high ground of Wales and the Southwest of England.

Other rather important mini-lows form as waves on cold fronts of established depressions (see page 31). They often do not develop much, but they stop the weather clearing from your locality for several hours in some cases and in summer they can become thundery. If the forecast goes for a cold front clearing from your area by a certain time and then the clearance does not come, then the reason is usually that a wave is rippling down the front, 'lifting' the weather back towards the north and west (NH) (or south and east (SH)). Eventually the cloud and rain clears, but it has taken much longer than the forecast would have led you to believe.

It is no good blaming the forecasters as where and when these waves will develop is quite problematic and there is no way of predicting many of them in advance. Some waves grow into new secondary depressions and these may be seen by the computer or recognised by the human forecaster from his experience with perhaps a hunch that a falling barometer recorded on some ship out to the west, when all those who surround it are showing no such signs, actually can be relied on to indicate the first formation of a new wave low.

Secondary depressions are, as they say, lows which form on the edge of a primary low. They can be vicious and more intense than the primary low and they can set up gales very rapidly when at the time it might appear that the skies are clearing and the wind is slackening.

Not all depressions need to form on the Polar Front or as waves on cold fronts. Some nasty lows come down as frontless whirls of cold air that are fully of heavy showers and even unseasonal snow. They are called 'polar lows' in Britain and they need an unusual situation with high pressure stuck to the west or northwest so as to bring a swathe of cold air down over the country. A similar situation off the west coast of North America with an immobile high over the Pacific results in outbreaks of cold air being driven right down across the United States and into the usually warm Southern States.

Which introduces us to the two kinds of anticyclone or high that exist. Anticyclones usually travel or they block, and travelling highs are normally relatively small in extent sometimes being merely ridges of high pressure stuck, as short periods of good weather, between the travelling lows. The blocking highs are however quite different. They break up the run of the circumpolar westerly winds and may sit more-or-less immobile over a vast tract of land or water for weeks and, in some spectacular cases, months on end.

When that happens we have to envisage the blocking high as a great ship anchored in the mainstream of the westerlies and so diverting them either side of it. Of course the depressions go where the westerlies go and when southern climes (NH) (or northern climes (SH)) experience unseasonal weather than a blocking anticylone is usually to blame. Equally, heat waves appear when blocking highs stick to the east of a locality. A wonderful Whitsun holiday week in Britain in 1982 came about because of high pressure stuck over central Europe. Temperatures soared towards the 90s F (30s C) as air was drawn across southern Europe from the Mediterranean region. Those who went to Spain for their Whitsun break had rain and cold.

We have to realise that even when the weather map looks almost the same for tomorrow as today the conditions for sailing may be very different. The weather map does not necessarily show if it will be cloudy or bright and even when a forecast indicates what cloud cover there will be it is very often variable from one place to another. The wind regime for sailing alters appreciably when the sun breaks through or conversely when sunny periods are followed by total overcast. What these changes are will be covered in Chapter 21.

14 Wind Shifts in a Run of Unsettled Weather

When a string of depressions chase one another across your area then they cannot do so without a ridge of high pressure forming in between. An idealised, but nevertheless instructive run of such weather is depicted in Fig. 9.1 where we have taken it that you are either somewhere to the south of the line along which the low centre will track (A-A) or to the north of it (B-B). You have to imagine that you are either at A or B on the right and that the weather situation depicted on the time scale arrives over you a day, two days etc. after some initial time (O).

Firstly we find ourselves in a fresh northwesterly that is blowing in behind one of the string of depressions. Let us concentrate on A. There will very likely be showers at first, but as the wind backs towards W and lightens, the air sinking from high up over the ridge of high pressure will damp out the showers and only fair weather Cu cloud will remain. Maybe half a day later the axis of the ridge passes and after a calm period the wind will gently pick up from S or SE.

Next day the upper cloud that foretells a warm front will be arriving overhead even though the wind is not much stronger. It does not change direction much either as the rain comes ahead of the warm front, but increases in speed. There is a fairly sharp shift to SW as the warm front passes and a bit of an increase, but not very much.

The next major shift is when the cold front comes along and then the wind veers to around NW and temporarily strengthens to 30 knots. However, it soon moderates to 20 knots and two days later we are back in another ridge.

Now let us follow the fortunes of B. In general the winds to the north of depression centres tend to be lighter than they are to the south and so while the wind at first is NW as it was at A, it is 5 knots lighter. However, the shifts as the ridge passes are the same as for A. It is when we get under the influence of the low, a day or more later, that there is a distinctly different pattern of wind shifts than were experienced at A. The wind goes from SE through NE to become N and later, after two days have passed, NW as the next ridge moves in.

The shifts experienced at A and B are both 'cyclonic' but the consistent southerly aspect of the wind ahead of the depression and the weather that comes with it confirms to those who cannot see a weather map (or in some other way find out what is happening) that the centre will pass to the north and that there will therefore be a set of veering shifts which come more-or-less sharply as fronts pass.

The initial SE wind that backs E and then NE will confirm that the low centre is tracking to the south. Also, while there will be Ci and other high clouds to be seen on the track B-B they may not mean that any rain will occur. It depends entirely on how near to the centre you are and how active the low is anyway. The 'cyclonic' backing wind indicates very often that it will eventually back further, but normally before the wind has backed as far as NW or W the skies have cleared and it is evident that another ridge of high pressure is coming in.

We see that while the 'anticyclonic' shift pattern is a fairly consistent backing from somewhere around NW or W to SE or S, with a very light phase somewhere between, what the cyclonic pattern is depends on where you are with respect to the track of the low. So having looked at what must happen when ridges and lows pass it should be possible for the dinghy or board sailor to make some predictions as to what is likely to happen to the wind in the longer term and act accordingly.

15 Fronts and Wind Shifts

Fronts

It is important to recognise the cloud types that form along fronts if you are going to assess in any coherent way when wind shifts are likely to occur. Because it is a wedge of warm moist air lying over cooler air, the warm front will throw out intelligence that it is coming up to a day ahead of it actually passing at the surface (Fig. 15.1).

The first recognisable signs of a coming warm front may be cirrus (Ci) clouds progressively invading the sky. They will have a characteristic hooked shape when they first appear, but may well become so numerous as to lie in banners and bands across the sky. In the latter case, and if at the

Figure 15.1 *A 3-D portrait of the clouds, fronts and isobars of a developing depression*

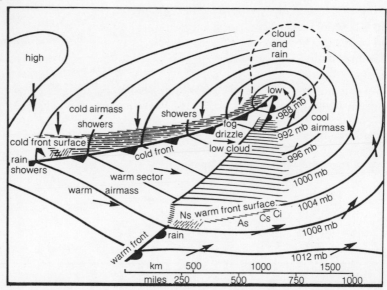

same time it is quite obvious to you that as high as they are the cirrus clouds are moving fast from northwest, then anticipate a day off from racing tomorrow because there is very likely to be a gale.

You will often be aware of these early signs of trouble through the gaps in fair-weather cumulus clouds, but there will not usually be any other cloud between the Cu and the Ci above it. Cirrus takes on many forms and sometimes it can mean nothing very much. On other occasions it appears for a time when the weather is going to improve rather than get worse – the meaning Ci usually has.

'Mackerel sky and mares' tails make tall ships carry low sails', says the weather lore and this connection between Ci clouds and bad weather has been recognised for centuries if not millennia.

Looking at the probable time-scale shown in Fig. 15.2. it is obvious that Ci seen gathering in the morning does not usually mean a major change of air mass today. What it does suggest is that the wind should be noticeably from a more westerly point by tomorrow and almost certainly it will be stronger. That does not mean however that there will not be very major changes in the wind today. It has already been pointed out that ahead of coming depressions – and that means warm fronts or occlusions as they are part of depressions – the wind must be expected to back and increase when the low centre is going to track north of you. This case is the most prevalent one on the coasts of Atlantic Europe except in the more northern countries, because most of the lows track out of the Atlantic and curve up towards Scandinavia. It will be the most likely situation in the United States where many lows track across Canada on their way into the Atlantic. As most lows track south of Australia and South Africa so in the SH the wind should veer and increase at first and then, later, back progressively as the fronts pass.

So NH sailors must expect a backing wind as the clouds gather and later a wind increase which may be slow in coming. Any shift into the southern quadrants should always make you think of a deteriorating weather situation.

You may not however see the Ci clouds when you get up in the morning. They may have already passed and you may now have the second cloud type

Figure 15.2 *A cross-section through the fronts and warm sector of a depression showing typical times when characteristic clouds etc. will be seen both ahead of the warm front and behind the cold front*

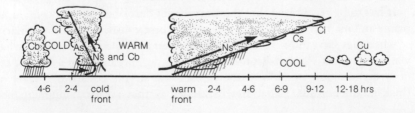

73

that comes in ahead of depressions. This is cirrostratus (Cs), easily recognisable when a ring halo appears around the sun (or moon).

'When the sun is in his house it will rain soon', says the weather lore and very often this is true, but in Britain – and probably elsewhere as well – only on two-thirds of the occasions that haloes are seen does rain follow. Still, met.-wise that is a fair score and if the wind is beginning to pick up from some southerly point as well, you can believe it. It is during this time that cumulus clouds begin to die out and below the white veil of Cs the whole airspace is clear of cloud.

The word 'soon' in the weather lore above usually means about six hours or more and so Cs seen around breakfast-time will indicate rain that afternoon, but before the rain starts the clouds will have to darken and thicken so that the sun will usually be lost slowly just as if it were disappearing behind thick ground glass. This indicates the cloud-type altostratus (As), which is a more-or-less uniform layer of moderately high cloud that is almost featureless and may even resemble mud-flats suspended inverted in the sky. The time when rain will occur is now much nearer and the wind should already be taking, or have taken, a tendency to increase with time. Typical wind speeds are Force 4 or even 5–6 at this stage.

It does not actually rain out of As cloud, but the increase in wind that occurs and the loss of the previous bright sky can have a lowering effect on morale. If you start under these conditions it may well be raining by the end of an extended race and, more importantly, the wind will probably have increased a Beaufort force or more. This follows because when rain starts in earnest there is nearly always an increase in wind at the same time and probably a slight veering shift as well (backing in SH).

Although technically rain does not occur from altostratus cloud, when it does start to rain it may not be highly noticeable that anything much has changed in the clouds above. The much thicker layers which result in rain are called nimbostratus (Ns) and to be correct we must call it As before it rains and Ns when it rains. As the rain starts to fall so does the cloud-base and while there will not be much change in the visibility the damp overcast will make the conditions seem much worse than they actually are. 'You can stand five more knots when the sun shines' is a very true adage.

Apart from increasing in speed not much will happen to the wind until the front actually passes. It is now that you can begin to consider what you will do if and when the wind comes from a more westerly point. General tactics for large-scale veering shifts are covered in Chapter 16.

It has to be recognised that the warm front described above is one in its prime and many fronts are not at all in their first youth. This is particularly so when they have moved a long way from their birthplace. Sometimes what was once a great vigorous frontal system has degenerated into a modest set of layers of cloud which near the surface will simply consist of a layer of thick stratocumulus. What has happened is that air from high up has subsided and eroded the high clouds leaving only the lowest layers which are now no longer thick enough to produce anything other than a spot or two of drizzle. These fronts are called kata fronts as they are the result of sinking air (compare katabatic winds that blow downhill). The young vigorous kind are called ana fronts (again compare anabatic winds) where most of the air is ascending and leading to more cloud and precipitation.

The problem is that often these old fronts will not be mentioned or even indicated in forecasts, but they can still have a wind shift under them and produce a change of air type. However, the shift may well only be fully complete after an hour or two has passed and when a bank of cloud moves in over you during a race and the wind shifts either steadily or in fits and starts over a period of time then a kata front is often responsible.

Behind warm fronts the air is warm, which often means it is also moist. Therefore as warm fronts pass we expect rain and low cloud to be followed by more cloud, but no rain. That is what often happens but in highland and steep coastal districts an on-shore warm wind grows cloud very easily, leading to very low cloud, drizzle and rain and sometimes fog. Otherwise the warm sectors of depressions may, in the summer half of the year, break up into very hot days, but cloudy nights. Warm sectors may well grow thunderstorms when the heat grows too unbearable.

Just as with warm fronts, cold fronts may go from being one of the most virile of weather systems to being almost nothing due to subsidence. However, once again we describe the young vigorous cold front and let the reader rub out its worst features as it becomes spent with time.

A cold front is a warm front in reverse, but it clears twice as fast as a warm front. It is also more violent in its air motions. While the ascent of air up a warm front surface is slow, with cold fronts it is often 'explosive' leading to squalls and heavy showers mixed with more general rain that will tail off with time in direct contrast to the warm front where the rain starts light and gradually increases in intensity. However, showeriness is not an attribute of warm fronts. Having said which, such fronts can become thundery when they advance over hot ground in the summer.

The cold front does not give hours of warning of its approach and the remarks on page 78 should be read here so that the imminent arrival of a cold front and its attendant wind shift can be recognised.

Both warm fronts and cold fronts can develop small wave lows on them, but they are much more prevalent on cold fronts and cause extended periods of rain when a relatively short period is to be expected (see Chapter 13). The cloud sequence as a cold front passes is shown in Fig. 15.2 and we must expect it to be followed by, if not a showery airstream, at least one which is full of heap clouds by day over land but which has clear skies by night.

Occluded fronts are produced as a depression runs through the middle reaches of its life cycle and they come about because cold fronts move faster than warm ones. Thus the former is always overhauling the latter and when this happens the warm air is lifted off the ground altogether.

The result from a sailing point of view is that instead of the frontal wind shifts coming in two distinct bands they come together with no distinct break. The chance of an occlusion producing a slow veer rather than a sharp one is high because of the length of time the fronts have been in existence. Ways of recognising occlusions include:

i early on as the high clouds come in they may be full of holes or open spaces showing that the front to come is not a true ana front,

ii when the rain has been going on for some time there may be a change that includes sudden showeriness in what has been an otherwise steady downpour. This is unusual with warm fronts and indicates that a cold front has followed a warm one without a break between.

Before leaving fronts a word about the real atmosphere. The theories of fronts lead us to conclude that what has been said above is the normal state of affairs. Sometimes, while the general character of the weather is such as to make you believe that a certain kind of front is passing, it may do so in odd ways. Several mini-fronts may seem to pass, each with a minor shift of wind; or what looks like a front passes with no shift of wind at all. These kinds of things happen, but they are much rarer than the normal way in which fronts act so the answer is to learn to recognise the normal situations and when the others occur take them as one of those met. things that happen now and again, but for which there is no explanation.

16 Recognising Frontal Wind Shifts

The wind always shifts clockwise (NH) across a true front no matter whether it is a warm front, a cold front or an occluded front. If the rain is falling steadily, the cloud lowers and the dark mien of the sky continues to convince you that a front is about to pass, then the front you have is either a true warm front or the warm front part of an occlusion. In either case the thing you are looking for is a line of raggedy cloud hanging in dark wisps below the cloud-base and usually silhouetted against a brighter sky to windward.

If the sky *is* brighter then that signifies a warm front and not an occlusion for in the latter case the warm front turns into a cold front without a break between. Yet even here there will normally be a darker, dirtier-looking line of cloud, probably lower than the rest, moving in on you from windward which lies more-or-less over the veering shift.

Possibly the new wind is going to come suddenly, maybe more slowly and only you on the spot can make up your mind about that. Sometimes you may not be able to assess whether the wind has shifted or not even though there has been a cessation of rain, a lifting of the cloud-base or even a break to clearer skies. If the wind has not shifted appreciably then expect that this is a trough which has run on ahead of the true frontal shift or shifts.

I say shifts because older fronts, which have travelled some way over land, or over a variety of terrains, may pass fully only after several mini-fronts have passed. I remember one occasion sailing down on the South Coast of England when it was possible to recognise the passing of no less than three phases and each time the wind shifted a little more to the west and eventually to WNW. It all went by in less than an hour and during this time the cloud would grow dark and then lighten and there would be a shift only to close in again before the next lighter patch came along with its bit of wind shift etc.

It is very important from a practical point of view to recognise that fronts, which look like sharp lines on the weather map, may be anything but sharp lines of change in practice. They are most likely to be sharp on oceanic coasts that face the prevailing winds, but they become progressively more smudged as they proceed into a land mass. Some of this smudging is due to the frictional effect of the land on the surface air which gets dragged back under the on-rushing frontal air above so that the latter topples over onto the ground. Something like a wave breaking on a surf beach, but maybe a thousand times bigger (I have indicated this in Fig. 15.2).

With cold fronts you have no build-up of cloud ahead to warn of their coming. The forecast will often warn of a cold front passing through the area sometime during the time you are sailing, but as the timing of met. variations is the most difficult thing to get right so you will be left to keep your own weather eye to windward to assess when, if at all, the front is going to be upon you.

You have to have warm air ahead of a cold front because remember the air behind the front gives its name to the front.

So if colder air is to come, warmer air must be with you now. The attributes of warm air masses have already been outlined in Chapter 13. Thus we expect it to be warm and humid with a great deal of cloud around the sky, maybe a total cover of low cloud which can be dark and lumpy due to turbulent overturnings as the wind bowls over the terrain. Or perhaps there will be a simple fog-like layer at low level straight in off the sea and covering the higher ground inland. This is stratus and such cloud, which persists on a coast facing the wind, may well break up and give a hot day inland.

When the maritime Tropical air is less wet it often forms layers of stratocumulus which have an undulating base that is quite high up compared to layers like stratus. Stratocumulus is, as it says, a layer of lumps spread around the sky and is usually associated with not much change. However, that may be bad intelligence when the next thing to spring out of the west is a cold front.

Sometimes you will be able to see the grey and white wall of cloud sweeping down on you and you can then act accordingly. At other times clouds you already have may obscure the coming front until it is on top of you, but only on the rarest occasions does a cold front not give you warning of its coming. There will be a dark pall thrown over the water and squall marks on it to windward as well as the sign of the unwary being blown over or at least having to meet an increased wind. It can be that the first herald is big spots of rain, for the cold front rain starts heavy and gets lighter with time in direct contrast to the warm front rain that does exactly the opposite. However, most cold fronts produce sharper, more showery conditions as they pass. There can be some thunder and a peal of thunder in the winter as the rain lashes the windows is a pure sign that a sharp cold front is blowing by.

The fronts which will produce sharp, almost instantaneous, wind shifts show this by odd-looking, contrary motions in the clouds that are just about

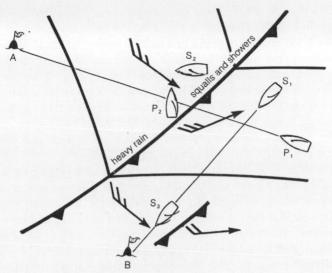

Figure 16.1 *The effect of a cold front wind shift on boats beating on starboard (S) and port (P) tacks just ahead of the shift. Starboard tack S_1 can simply round up to meet the new wind (S_2). Port tack P_1 will be headed by the squalls, may lose way and capsize. Anyway the new port tack course P_2 is a disadvantage if making for A. In the case of S_1 making for B, the front has been moved on in time as shown at S_3*

to cross you. Expect a squall and meet it by getting onto starboard tack (NH) (port tack SH) so that you can round-up into the squall (S_1–S_2) and not be put in irons as may well happen when a veering shift (backing SH) comes in on port tack (P_1–P_2) (Fig. 16.1).

Contrary cloud motions, squalls, dark roll-like features in the immediate clouds etc. all spell that a sharp wind shift is upon you. Usually of course the wind is Force 5 or more as well because if a weather feature is to pass quickly it must be driven by strong winds. If there is only about Force 3–4 ahead of the front then expect Force 5–6 or more for a time behind it.

Another help in assessing the severity of a coming cold front is from the forecasts. If they are going for heavy showers to follow the front this indicates a colder and more unstable air mass than normal. The sharper the contrast between the temperature of the air ahead and behind the front the sharper and more vicious the front will be. It is also important to realise that frontal troughs may shift the wind through very big angles – over 90° sometimes.

In Fig. 16.1 the effect of such a shift can be assessed. Two situations where the course to a mark is a beat before the front passes and shifts the wind are as shown. In going for Mark A a dinghy (P_1) was beating on port and the shift will turn that into a beat on starboard (S_2). The way the isobars kink shows that the wind may be say Force 6 ahead and only Force 4 behind (although in another situation it could be the exact opposite).

If making for Mark B it would be a beat on starboard ahead of the frontal shift which will become a broad reach on the same tack as the wind swings onto the starboard quarter (S_3). That could be the more hairy situation as the wind comes more-or-less suddenly from abaft the beam and the squalls that accompany the showers make nonsense of the general run of the isobars that are only Force 4. The wind will become more representative as and when the heavier rain tails off, but for now all is wet and windy and screaming planes are the order of the day.

Since with an occluded front there is no warm sector, the only way to be sure that the warm front you think is passing at this moment is in fact an occlusion, is when the steady rain turns showery. Even then you cannot always be sure that the warm front has not been modified and is producing showery-type rain before it clears. However, the latter event is rare.

The wind shift across an occlusion zone is often going to be one of the slower affairs because the older fronts become the more chance there is that they will pass in a broad zone of changes rather than one quick short-lived shift. You can be pretty sure that what you have had is an occluded front when the steady rain typical of warm fronts changes to rain mixed with heavier bursts of showery rain and then the whole thing tails away as the cloud lifts. Often the length of time all this takes to go by is considerably less than the usually accepted times for more active warm and cold fronts separately.

17 Introducing Places to Sail – Inshore Sailing

From a weather and wind point of view the sailing venues can be broadly divided up as shown in Fig. 17.1. If you sail straight off a beach onto the open sea or if you engage in Olympic-style courses set out in the ocean or in the middle of bays or similar, in fact anywhere where you are at the mercy of the sea, your problems will differ from those who sail in the cosier confines of a creek, river or reservoir.

Because of the prevalence of seabreeze effects and the way they act, these *Inshore* waters and the roughly 3-mile (5-kilometre) wide strip of land next to the sea coast – what we will call the *Beachlands* – are very likely to be modified in spring and summer by seabreeze forces. Thus in the Beachlands we will include lagoons and étangs plus harbours, creeks and estuaries which are within this relatively narrow throw of the main sea coast.

Again, mainly because of the modifications introduced by the seabreeze forces, we are going to call the next seven miles or so the *Coastlands* and here again long arms of the sea, rivers and coastal lakes and reservoirs will be included. Beyond the 10-mile limit we are, from a seabreeze point of view, *Inland*, and now this will be the preserve of the river sailors, and the denizens of gravel-pits, lakes and reservoirs.

The last major division we need to make is one we shall call *Highland*. This does not mean that only finger lakes lost between craggy mountains will qualify for the title of 'Highland' waters. Anywhere where there is some elevation and the wind has come to you via sizeable hills or over a substantial ridge, or is set to leeward of a mountain area, may be termed highland. The kind of waters involved may be lochs, or fiords at sea level, but when they get confined, so that the wind has to take very considerable note of the lie of the land, then that is for us *Highland* waters.

There may be places which do not fit these categories, but we have to limit ourselves or this book will become vastly too long.

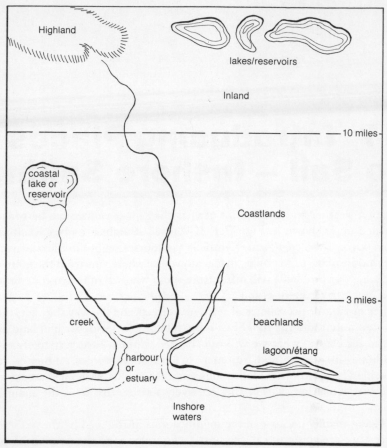

Figure 17.1 *Because of the way the wind behaves – especially the seabreeze – the sailing venues will be divided as in this diagram*

Inshore Sailing

When you sail inshore you have certain problems that will not arise in other venues. The biggest one is that of sea and swell. After a blow has subsided the wind may have decreased to a quite gentle Force 3 to 4 or even less, but the swell left by the storm continues to run so that you are lost temporarily in the troughs and keeping an eye on distant marks of the course becomes difficult. Add a seaway to the swell and locating marks becomes such a major preoccupation that a deck-compass becomes almost a necessity. You may also start off saturated by having to launch through the surf and so a wet-suit would be a good idea if it is not a boiling hot day. Seas grow at the same time as the wind grows with no perceptible time-lag between them and a race inshore which starts off in almost calm conditions may easily end up in relatively rough conditions. The opposite may not however be true because if you start in rough conditions and the wind suddenly subsides, the swell is still there even if the seaway is not.

On pleasant mornings with light off-shore winds, *Inshore* is where the seabreeze will start and so race committees can expect great calm patches to settle on these waters and frustrate starts in the forenoon. What will happen to the wind on such mornings depends entirely on where the wind is blowing from compared to the lie of the coast (Fig. 17.2). When the wind blows too strongly for a proper seabreeze to develop, the afternoon off the beaches may well be the place with least wind anywhere. In these circumstances the wind goes down with the afternoon as the seabreeze forces strive against the off-shore wind and then it strengthens again in the evening. This is a case contrary to the diurnal variation outlined on page 83, and it is seen at its strongest along the high Adriatic coast where the mountain wind falls onto the *Inshore* waters in the early morning, making for maximum wind speed around 10 a.m., only to be met later in the day by the seabreeze forces acting towards the sunlit mountain slopes. Thus a minimum wind speed develops around the middle of the day, and the afternoon when there ought to be most wind, finds least wind. Later in the evening the wind comes back again as the seabreeze forces falter with the onset of night.

Do not imagine that this effect can only be felt in places with strong local winds like the Mediterranean. I recall an overcast morning at Poole Bay in Dorset on the South Coast of England which grew bright as the stronger summer sun ate up the tops of the clouds, but where the sun never actually broke through. Although no direct sun came out on the coast the cloud broke up inland and there was enough heat through the thinning overcast to

Figure 17.2 *For our purposes the wind directions will be classified as shown here*

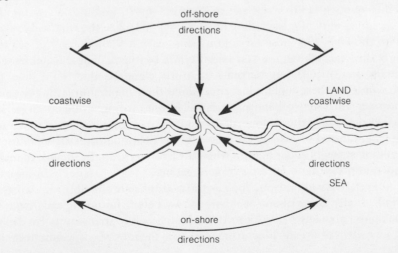

produce a seabreeze force against the off-shore wind that was only about 10 knots in the morning and fell progressively as time went on so that it was only 5 knots or less in the afternoon. Olympic-style courses had been laid in the Bay, but the races had to be abandoned as even the leaders ran out of time.

When the wind is going down with time then being a leader of a one-design class or the long, fast members of a handicap class is always an advantage because the average wind speed for the course is obviously greater the shorter the time involved on the course. Here is where evening races will nearly always favour the long dinghies and the catamarans as the wind falls progressively with the sun. Tidal streams whose speed changes appreciably within an hour or so can affect this rule, but exceptions are rare on the open sea because the speed of tidal ebbs and floods are not normally as great as in tidal arms of the sea. However, in handicap racing those further back can gain advantage from a tidal set that is adverse and is getting less with time, though even then it is necessary that the last of the racing should be around and following half tide when the stream is strongest and so changing most rapidly with time.

Now let us consider winds that blow almost along the coastline. These will be turned to have components on-shore by the daytime seabreeze forces even if they are too strong to allow of being shifted into a true seabreeze. For example a northerly wind blowing down an east-facing coast, which of course sees the full sun from early morning, and which freshens during the day to Force 5 or 6, will be found to be from around NNE close inshore. Thus when beating, inshore legs will be helped by holding on as close to the beach as possible and the effect may on occasions be such as to allow a very long haul along the beach on these starboard legs, especially when indentations cause the coastline to temporarily bear away inland.

Where the coastline rises cliff-like out of the sea never underestimate the ability of such land to channel the wind along it, and also allow for the unpredictability of gusts falling off the cliff-tops when the wind is blowing from the land. On those rare sunny days with a shallow layer of sea fog shrouding everything, the best visibility will be found along those cliffs that see the sun since the up-currents there will clear the fog.

Inshore is where night wind effects find their maximum. It is the early morning when such off-shore winds will be felt by dinghy and board sailors as they depend on the coolness of the high slopes inland to propel the denser air downhill and so out over the coast. It is rare to find nocturnal wind forces building strongly enough, even when the land rises rapidly inland, to make much impression on evening *Inshore* sailing.

Off relatively low coasts, such as the South Coast of England, the night wind usually starts about an hour or two before midnight and finds its maximum about two o'clock in the morning before dying away by dawn.

When winds already blow from the shore then the night wind effect can help to keep things going up to and after dark, but as very few dinghy or board sailors relish the thought of bashing about after dark we are going to ignore this period of the day.

Equally, winds that blow on-shore in the morning will be aided by seabreeze forces and relatively light morning winds with not much seaway can become fresh or even strong by afternoon with the aid of the sun on the land.

18 The Seabreeze Inshore

When you sail on the open sea and the weather is fair the changes of wind engendered by seabreeze forces will be more complicated than in almost any other venue. It is here, in the first few miles from the shoreline, that the seabreeze first makes its effects felt, but what subsequently happens depends on the wind direction and speed in the early part of the day. So if you want to gain ideas about wind shifts that are likely to occur later in the day then breakfast-time is when you should make a real effort to assess the true state of the wind. Hints on this are to be found on page 110.

We can make a quick first appraisal of the situations that develop in the following way. Referring to Fig. 17.2, we have to use the main run of the coastline as a reference direction and if your bit of coast is very indented and broken by bays and promontories then you may find that these ideas will not work too well. Where they work best is where the coast is relatively low and straight for some tens of miles in either direction, and we must remember that it needs to be sunny, fair or bright over the land before the seabreeze force can build up to affect the wind over the inshore waters.

Divide the circle of wind directions into:

  i on-shore: the least complicated situation,
 ii off-shore: the most complicated situation,
iii coastwise: where seabreeze forces will try to bend the wind landward.

On-shore Situation

If it is cloudy over land and sea and the cloud does not break or become thin then the wind will not change due to thermal influences.

If there are heap clouds over the sea this shows the air is cool compared to the sea and will be even cooler compared to the land later in the day. This situation generates wind increase over inshore waters as the day progresses and Force 3 to 4 in the morning can easily become 5 to 6 in the afternoon. It can also become gusty and as the waves grow with the wind so a smooth or slight sea will become moderate or more by afternoon. This is situation (a)

86

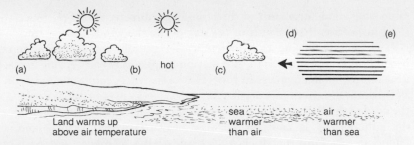

Figure 18.1 *Things that happen near the coast when the wind is on-shore:*
(a) normal sunny conditions with Cu clouds – strengthened wind
(b) hot cloudless conditions – sluggish wind
(c) Cu over the sea when sea warmer than the air
(d) low cloud when air warmer than the sea
(e) no cloud when air warmer than the sea

in Fig. 18.1 and we can expect heap clouds to build over the land with the seabreeze forces helped on by sun shining through gaps between them and the general impetus that the growth of heap clouds gives to them.

If there is a layer of stratus (fog-like) cloud hanging over the sea this indicates that the air is warmer than the sea and when this layer gets ashore it will 'burn off' and the day will become hot and probably humid (Situations (b) and (d)). Seabreeze forces do not do well on such days and so while there will probably be some form of pick-up in the wind speed by the afternoon it will not be marked (Situation (b)).

If the wind is light the stratus may be down on the sea surface itself and so be fog. This fog probably does not exist very far inland and in any case will go as the sun gets up. However, there are mornings, especially in spring when the sea is cold, when fog-banks off the coast will be drawn in from seaward as the seabreeze starts up over the coastline. Unfortunately, at this time of year the fog blankets the previously warming land and so kills the seabreeze force. Now the cold, clammy fog just settles over land and water and ruins what promised to be a very nice day.

Intermediate conditions of cloud which are neither really heap nor of an amorphous layer type may not tell you much about what will happen, but in general broken higher layers of cloud over the sea will not affect the situation ashore. So well-broken altostratus and altocumulus islands dotted about the sky must indicate increasing wind by afternoon whereas the onset of frontal cloud will also indicate increasing wind, but this time built by the tightening of the pressure pattern.

So most conditions of broken cloud or of little or no cloud over the land as you go to the clubhouse in the morning will lead you to expect that the on-shore wind you now have will increase later in the day, and correspondingly die back in strength during the evening. You must at the same time allow for a shift of direction more directly on-shore, especially right inshore as the warmth of the day draws the wind.

It is as well to note that in temperate latitudes the seabreeze forces become very weak in autumn, but they build quickly in early spring to reach a maximum of effectiveness in June. However, where cold water exists off a steepish coastline for most of the year, as occurs say in the Gulf of Bothnia at the head of the Baltic, the seabreezes become a major factor for the whole of the summer. It is contrast between sea-surface temperature and air temperature ashore that fuels the engine of the seabreeze and northern latitudes help this situation. We must include here big lakes and reservoirs whose south-facing slopes will always be candidates for the generation of on-shore breezes when other wind conditions allow.

Off-shore Situation

Here the seabreeze effects are most rewarding of study, but are also inevitably the most complex. Having said which it is not difficult to understand the situation that develops over inshore waters on the mornings of seabreeze days.

The first couple of miles of travel of an off-shore wind over the cool sea on a fair morning, leads to the air sinking. At the same time the upward expansion of the air over the heated land produces an outflow of air to the sea at altitude. The latter effect lowers the pressure ashore compared to that over the sea (which does not change appreciably). This pressure difference builds as the sun rises higher and by 11 a.m. (sun-time) or so, it is sufficient to have reduced much of the inshore venue to calm or fitful light airs (Fig. 18.2).

Over the water, surface-hugging air is drawn in towards the beach. This layer may initially be so shallow as not to reach above the gunwale, but once it finds itself over the warm beach it rises as convection currents. This gives a sudden impetus to the whole system and air begins to blow from seaward in greater and greater amounts. Now you get the first true wind you may have had for an hour or more and once you have recognised that the sea-breeze system is working, expect it to go on working and strengthening and sail accordingly.

If you are far out you will still have the off-shore wind while further inshore there is calm or the seabreeze has begun to blow. If you see boats becalmed inshore or sailing in an on-shore wind while you have an off-shore one, then you will have to allow for the temporary passage of a calm zone as the seabreeze system strengthens its grip on the winds over the whole of the coast.

To help envisage what is happening and what will happen, we can use an idea I first put forward in the *Wind Pilot* (Nautical Publishing). Think of the coming seabreeze as wrapped up in the rolls of a 'seabreeze carpet' (Fig. 18.3). At first a small length of the carpet gets pulled out towards the shore

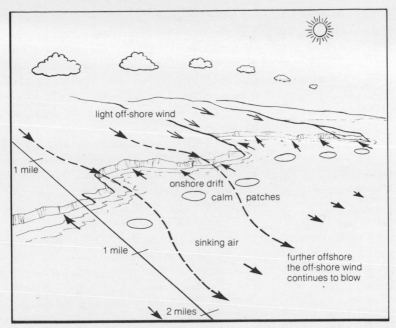

Figure 18.2 *The situation over inshore waters on the morning of a seabreeze day with an off-shore wind*

(a). The carpet roll is envisaged as being where the zone of calm is. Beyond it, further to seaward, the off-shore wind continues to blow just as it does over the land. With time the carpet is pulled out over the beaches and where it is laid, the seabreeze blows (b). However, another thing that the seabreeze carpet helps you visualise is how the calm zone (or antifront) moves seawards at the same time as the carpet itself is being laid further and further inland with the day. By the afternoon of a good day the 'roll' has gone perhaps twenty or more miles seaward while the carpet stretches perhaps thirty miles inland and sometimes more.

Like all analogies we must not push it too far. The wind arrows are not fixed to the surface of the carpet, but blow over it faster than it itself is being laid. The extra speed is allowed for when we realise that inland, at the carpet's edge, there are updraughts into a line of heavier clouds that constitute the seabreeze front. We shall need to say more about this front when we describe the seabreeze over Beachland, Coastland and Inland venues. For now, looked at from the point of view of the Inshore sailor, the seabreeze front is a means by which his seabreeze current can continue to blow, constantly being fed by sinking air over the sea and returned again aloft along the seabreeze front. Apart from that, it is usually beyond his ken.

However, do not lose sight of the fact that the wind you had this morning is probably still there inland trying to blow the seabreeze back out to sea.

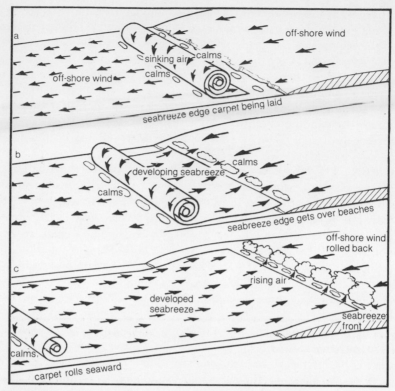

Figure 18.3 *The seabreeze carpet idea helps in understanding the complex wind changes that go on on many seabreeze days:*
(a) is the middle of the forenoon and is at a time just prior to the situation depicted in Fig. 18.2
(b) is when the edge of the seabreeze carpet is just getting ashore and the breeze is really beginning to pick up
(c) is the afternoon when a developed seabreeze is blowing to feed into a seabreeze front inland

Once the sun begins to lose its power the wind may begin to beat the breeze and the onset of a calm over waters which have enjoyed an afternoon of seabreeze, must make you think straight away about another wind reversal to come sooner or later. Without other information you can only assume that the overall pressure pattern is still much the same now as it was this morning before the seabreeze came in. In settled weather that is usually the case anyway. So remembering the original direction will help you cope with the return of the wind in the late afternoon or evening.

Once the seabreeze begins to falter or large 'holes' appear in it, keep an eye landward for the return of the wind. Sometimes it will be marked by a cloud edge coming at you from inland. Near that edge is a wind shift that can have what was windward transformed into leeward and vice versa. It does not always show itself with a cloud-line, but any cloudiness arriving over the sea heralds the death of the seabreeze. This follows because the sinking air currents over the sea that are necessary to feed the breeze also lead to clear skies there as well. So the invasion of this sunny prospect by low cloud from shoreward indicates a wind from that direction too.

The evening wind that replaces the breeze can be quite fresh at times, but it is more usual for the strength to be low and on many occasions the end to a seabreeze day is a flat calm over the *Beachlands* as well as over the *Inshore* venue.

On page 115 I have described the ding-dong battles that sometimes develops between wind and breeze over the beaches and occasionally further inland. It is therefore useful to realise that the effective 'beach' may be seaward of where you think it is as far as the seabreeze is concerned.

On page 92 we talk about the way warmed water from tidal creeks etc. can lay off the coast towards the end of the ebb. This often streams along the coastline and provides what I have chosen to call a 'phantom beach' over which the necessary convection 'chimney' can build. There may be no cloud over such a chimney, but it can still induce wind to blow into it from both sides.

Let us describe an actual case which occurred during a One-Ton cup race off the entrance to Chichester Harbour during a very hot summer. The boats were to start at 11 a.m. and were some four miles off the coast. At 10 a.m. it was flat calm, but then a wind began to blow from landward when, with brilliant sunshine there ought to have been a seabreeze drift *towards* the shore (Fig. 18.4).

Because the race committee saw the wind was from the land they laid the first leg to a mark inshore and they thought themselves vindicated when the wind increased to Force 3 and all the boats had a reasonable wind to get them round the inshore mark and through the two reaching legs of an Olympic triangle. However, at the leeward turning mark the leaders (*Windsprite* and *Chartreuse*) rounded the buoy and came to an abrupt halt in flat calm. These not very happy leaders became happier when the rest of the fleet also ran out of wind just a little before they reached the mark, so proving that the edge of the calm was advancing slowly shorewards. It was very frustrating to see the off-shore wind still blowing not very far shorewards. However, they could also see there was a light on-shore breeze developing to seaward of them. They were in fact lying becalmed under a seabreeze 'chimney' up which both winds were blowing.

The reason for this chimney being four miles seaward of where it might have been expected to be lay in the 'river' of very warm ebbing water that was streaming out of the entrance to the Harbour and turning to run down the Channel towards the Isle of Wight. Its warmth promoted the necessary convection currents and so provided a 'phantom beach'.

If you refer to the 'seabreeze carpet' idea of how the seabreeze system works (page 88) you will realise that this calm zone off the coast could have been mistaken for the seabreeze 'antifront'. However, the latter advances out to sea whereas this calm zone was moving *shorewards* proving that it was *the* seabreeze front itself. The calm zone was so narrow that a couple of leading boats were pushed to the landward side of it by the slight tidal stream so picking up the Force 3 off-shore wind and were soon on their way to finish. The rest hoisted spinnakers and drifted in roped to the seabreeze front as it progressed shorewards.

Many oddities of the wind in light conditions might be accounted for in the same way because in coastal shallows there can be very different temperatures between one body of water and another and it is my experience that only a slight difference in temperature is required to initiate a 'chimney' over the warmer parts or along lines of transition between warm and cold water. Into and up these chimneys the local wind will blow and if the warm water is extensive it can provide some quite reasonable wind speeds as is evident from this above example.

Before leaving this same One-Ton series let me describe another

Figure 18.4 *The One-Ton Cup course off the entrance to Chichester Harbour which was bedevilled by calms due to a 'phantom beach'. Insert (a) shows the positions as Windsprite and Chartreuse just broke clear*

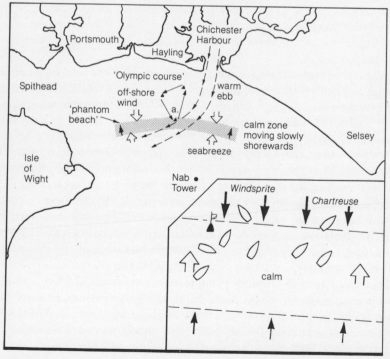

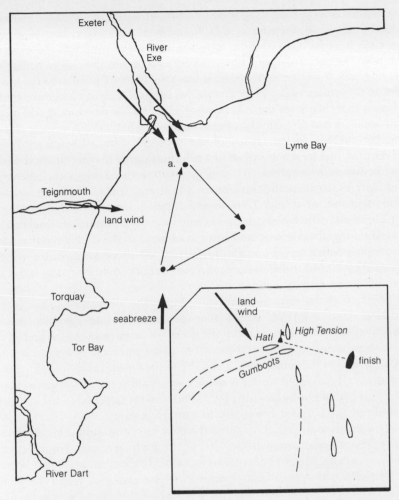

Figure 18.5 *The Olympic triangle course off Teignmouth for the final race of the One-Ton Cup series. Insert (a) shows how the three leading boats finished*

remarkable incident which proves that it pays to study the seabreeze. It was given to me (as was the one above) by Richard Creagh-Osborne, against whom I used to sail in the Firefly Class, and who usually used to sail his Firefly faster than I did! Richard, an Olympic protagonist, has now sadly been taken from us.

The race concerned was the last of the series and Richard was the tactician on *Gumboots* which needed something over 5 points to win the series. The Olympic triangle was laid off Teignmouth in Devon (Fig. 18.5) and due to a delayed start they were still racing on the final leg to the finish at four in the afternoon.

Creagh-Osborne said, 'The inland cumulus built up in the classic manner and the seabreeze started about 1100 and was very steady, but the crews were too busy with the in-fighting to notice that the wind was reducing in the final stages of the race. The seabreeze had taken the classic course of veering with the afternoon so that it was now blowing parallel to the coast and up the estuary of the River Exe. Thus the final leg was a long run before a breeze that *Gumboots'* crew were puzzled to find was developing odd puffs and holes'. Then Creagh-Osborne recognised what was happening. Here was the prelude to the return of the off-shore wind. They were lying eleventh at that time and began to work shorewards to meet the new wind that he was sure was about to come. No such tactic could go unchallenged and there were eventually three boats well shorewards of the direct course. The other two were *High Tension* and *Hati*.

Chartreuse, which had gained a commanding lead round the final mark, stayed on the direct course and ran out of wind in the calm zone that was developing between seabreeze and returning off-shore wind. Boats well to seaward continued to sail in the seabreeze, but of course gradually lost it as the calm zone moved seaward with time.

The fate of the race now lay with where the three boats, who were crossing courses inland, would manage to insert into the new wind. *Gumboots* led at that moment, but the other two were close behind and all of them were trying to estimate the exact moment when the new wind would arrive and what the course would then be to the finish. It was a tricky thing to fathom. If they went too far inshore they would get the wind earlier, but the course would be a slow run; too far off and the faster fetch to the mark would not make up for being late in gathering way.

Soon the dark strip that heralded the coming of the wind showed up inshore. It was maddeningly fickle, first pushing a finger here to nearly reach one boat, then dying, to be replaced by calm. In the fitful puffs that began to take effect, the three boats manoeuvred for position. When the wind finally came, *High Tension* was furthest inshore and the others were on a shorewards leg. Thus by luck *High Tension* got the wind first and sped off across the others who were tacking desperately in order to meet the new wind now that it was literally on top of them. *Hati* got it next and seizing her chance made a perfect set of her tall-boy to gradually close in on *Gumboots* who was denied the wind for a few precious seconds.

The end result was that *High Tension* came home ten lengths ahead of *Hati* who just got a nose ahead of *Gumboots*. The main body of boats that had stuck to the direct course had by then got the wind and their leader finished a length astern of *Gumboots*, but the latter had made eight points, more than enough for her to clinch the series. Thus that decision to seek the edge of the returning off-shore wind probably won *Gumboots* the series and it illustrates that there is a great deal to be gained from knowledge of the way the wind works in general and the seabreeze in particular.

Of course no one such incident can be said to win a sailing race. Only exemplary handling and pilotage over several races had put *Gumboots* and her crew in such a position that this correct use of wind tactics could clinch the series. On the other hand, had the right diagnosis of the situation not been made she could not have elevated herself to that undeniably best place to be – the overall winner of a very competitive class.

It is worth noting that because of the direction they face, certain coasts are not as likely to be noted for their seabreezes as others. Take the Channel coast of France. This faces either north or northwest. Thus the northerly wind directions, which most often bring convection and so active sea-breeze fronts, are on-shore directions for these coasts.

The off-shore directions are ones fed by winds from warm quarters around the Mediterranean and they will often be dry. Seabreeze fronts, and so seabreezes themselves, have difficulty in developing in such airstreams and so while we find the South and East coasts of Britain hailed as 'strong' seabreeze coasts the opposite coasts of Europe do not show the same numbers of seabreezes nor do they penetrate as far on many occasions. That does not mean that seabreezes do not occur. We know that they do and one of the strongest seabreezes I have ever encountered started up from flat calm in the Baie de la Seine and winged us into Le Havre in very fine style. However, the Baie is one of those 'funnels' for seabreeze that occur on most coastlines.

19 Effects Along the Coast

The veer effect

An important wind-shift effect that occurs when seabreezes start to blow in the morning and continue through the afternoon, is one due to the earth's rotation. Any wind that starts to blow in the temperate latitudes is, from the point of view of the observer, going to shift to the right of its original direction as time goes on (SH – it will shift to the left). As the seabreeze is a wind that starts to blow straight in over the coast and if it starts say at 10 a.m. (local sun time), then by 4 p.m. it has experienced a full six hours of the rotational veer. What has actually happened is that the breeze has remained blowing in the same direction in space, but you, the observer, have rotated under it as the time has gone on (Fig. 19.1).

In six hours, if at the Pole, the shift would be a full 90° and at the Equator

Figure 19.1 *The veer effect on the seabreeze (or any wind that starts suddenly and continues to blow). Here 4 hours of shift is illustrated at 50°N. You and the shore rotate with the earth, but the breeze blows in the same direction in space. To you south is still along a meridian, but the breeze is coming from SW*

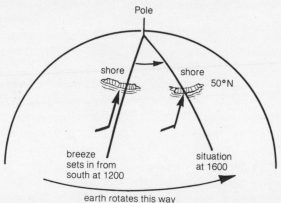

the effect is zero. In between these latitudes the degree of shift in six hours will vary from 0° to 90° as the latitude increases. Thus at 50°N the potential shift in six hours is about 70°.

The breeze may not always attain this shift, but it will tend towards it and an example has already been quoted on page 94. Thus on an east-facing coast the breeze will veer through SE during the afternoon; on a south-facing coast it will shift through SW while on a west-facing coast it will shift through NW. On a north-facing coast the inability of the sun to shine directly on the slopes of coastal hills can produce merely an increase in westerly winds and no true seabreeze. However, the veer effect will bring the coastwise wind on-shore and hence the afternoon onset of seabreezes.

When the Wind Blows Coastwise

It is a fairly normal occurence to have easterly winds blowing along the English Channel and this is an example of a coastwise wind direction, for the English coastline lies roughly E-W between Beachy Head and Torbay. However, all coasts change direction, sweeping into bays and out into promontories. Thus which one of the three sets of directions we have chosen will fit your situation is up to you to decide. Or keeping our example of the South Coast of England, the intervention of islands like the Isle of Wight provide beaches that face in all directions and where our east wind will be on-shore, off-shore and coastwise depending on where you are sailing.

With this in mind we will consider coastwise directions as shown in Fig. 17.2 and note that not all coastlines are the same when it comes to shifting the wind by thermal efforts. Coasts that look east see the sun early and keep it during the middle of the day and this applies even more to those that face southeast. They are very likely to produce the strongest influence on coastwise winds as the sun climbs high in the sky. Thus as in Fig. 19.2 a south-facing coast with an E wind at 11 a.m. (local sun time) may well have a SE wind close inshore by the afternoon and a course laid off the beaches with a first leg dead into the wind must be expected to favour the inshore starboard tack as time goes on. It may be quite nasty out there with comparatively big seas only made slightly more palatable by the sunshine, but the thermal influence can still bend the 20-knot wind even though the result could never be called a seabreeze as such.

If the wind is 10 knots or less then a full-scale seabreeze can result (temperate latitudes) by early afternoon. If it is around the top of Force 4 (16 knots) then a considerable on-shore cant can be induced in it even if no true seabreeze brings the wind in more directly from seaward. Above this speed only a bend can be expected and this will be relatively close to the shoreline.

This of course refers to the best seabreeze days with sunshine and heap clouds over the land. With cloudier but still bright conditions, or when the

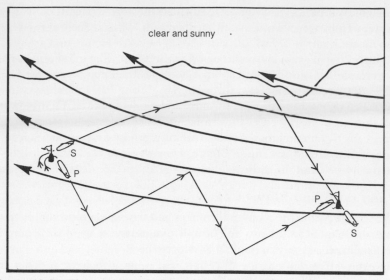

Figure 19.2 *The tactical use of the on-shore cant due to thermal influence produced in a coastwise wind of some strength. The board on starboard tack (S) who takes a long haul inshore ends up well ahead of the one who started on port (P) and sailed a conventional beating course*

cloud breaks late in the morning, there may only be enough force engendered to produce a shorewards cant in light to moderate winds.

The simple rule is to expect and look for the coastwise-blowing wind to develop on-shore cants during the day and to lose them again during the early evening. The tactical situation is shown in Fig. 19.2. Assuming the wind is blowing along the coast at 11 a.m. then by midday it can well have a noticeable shorewards cant and by 1–2 p.m. this can be enough to make it quite evident which is the quickest course from Mark A to Mark B. The figure also illustrates an important rule when beating:

If the wind is expected to shift to starboard – take starboard.

In this case the bent wind direction is expected to come from starboard of the original direct course and so on rounding A later in say a three-round race it pays to seek the expected shift by standing off inshore on starboard tack and holding the starboard legs as long as possible.

The direction a coast faces has a considerable effect on the wind that develops along it. An effect for which I must admit I do not have a convincing explanation is shown up by wind statistics from reliable stations on coasts that face north. It appears that the daytime trend is very often to increase W winds and this is what is shown to happen at places like Cherbourg, the north coast of Spain and the north-facing coasts of Germany, Poland etc. These three are the main north-facing coasts in Atlantic Europe; no extensive stretches occur in the USA for example.

The prevailing winds of the temperate latitudes are westerly and so your chances of sailing in a wind somewhere from the western quadrants is high. This means that south-facing coasts as well as north-facing ones are prime candidates to have winds from a coastwise direction. The trend is always to get back to that westerly direction and the seabreeze systems work best wherever there is shelter from the westerlies. Thus on the Baltic coasts we find that wherever a bay or gulf occurs, seabreezes occur frequently in the shelter of the promontories which slow down the west winds. The same can be said for the predominantly north-facing coast of France that faces the English Channel. Cherbourg gains more W winds with the day on a statistical basis, but the seabreezes blow well in the Baie de la Seine beyond it and the same can be said for the Gulf of St Malo, protected from the west by the quite high ground of Tregonrois. On the English coast Lyme Bay is well protected from the west by Dartmoor and the high ground that spreads southwards to Start Point. Seabreezes can start and go ashore here in circumstances where you might not expect them.

Whenever you look at the coastline of a venue you have never sailed before, note amongst other things how protected you are from the predominant westerlies. Not only will that make it more likely that the waves will not be a problem, but also it will tell of thermal winds to be considered. Out on the coasts that face the west and have no real shelter, waves can grow big and local thermal forces may not be much in evidence.

Effect of Seabreezes into Bays

Seabreezes are shallow winds and tend to blow round the higher promontories and headlands. Consider that since, as in Fig. 19.3, it is a seabreeze afternoon and the course is laid round four buoys in a bay that is partly enclosed by two fairly massive headlands you can expect the flow of the breeze to be rather like the diagram. In such diagrams wherever the streamlines pack together, there the wind is strongest and where they fan out, as they do inshore, there the wind will decrease somewhat.

Assume that the start is at A. As you have visualised how the streamlines will flow, you expect the wind to shift to port on the first part of the beat to B, so you take port (unless there is something which prevents it). You expect the headland to cut the wind speed in its lee and so you keep out clear of the end of the headland in anticipation of the wind bending to starboard round the headland where there ought to be more wind anyway. Assuming no tidal set you can go for the buoy B sooner than you might imagine as the wind going to starboard favours starboard.

The reach to C is just a reach and nothing more. The run from C to D is with wind that is going to shift to port as you go so take the port jibe in order to run at highest speed just off the dead run course.

If you carry a spinnaker the fastest way from D back to A is firstly to come up nearer the wind and get the boat in the reaching sector of its performance

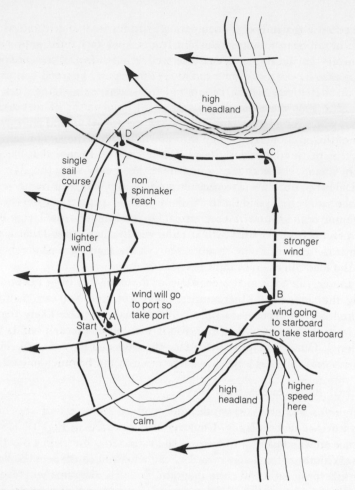

Figure 19.3 *A hypothetical race round four buoys in a bay into which a seabreeze (or other on-shore wind) is blowing*

diagram (page 181). This is then followed by a much broader spinnaker reach which Fig. 19.3 shows to be faster than the alternative direct course at 90° to the true wind.

Refraction and Other Effects

When sailing close inshore there are effects that can bend wind which has components either on-shore or off-shore. Firstly there is the universal tendency for the wind to flow more directly across the shoreline as shown in Fig. 19.4. The effect may not be as marked as depicted, but it can be when the shoreline is steep-to. As it is almost certainly due to the air trying to slide downhill we might call it the 'toboggan effect'.

Another is the so-called refraction effect. This depends on the relative roughness of land and water, but its effect is, I am sure, over-emphasised as it is a very small effect indeed. It is easy to show (*ref. Wind and Sailing Boats*) that for values of the ratio of speed over the water to that over the land up to $1\frac{1}{2}$, for example 18 knots over the water and 12 knots over the shore, the theoretical bending is about $10°$ in most practical situations. However, we have to ask ourselves, 'How far does the wind have to travel having broken clear of the shoreline before it gathers the enhanced speed?'

As the sheltering effect of the land on any adjacent water is well known it may be a long way from the shore before the new speed is gained and this extra speed has to pick up largely from the intervention of lumps of faster 'gradient' air coming down as gusts and speeding it up. If it is early morning or evening or the sky is overcast, the $10°$ shift may not be noticed as it might take a run of a mile or more before the wind fully realises its new speed.

Then there is another factor which has to be taken into account. Winds over the land blow across the isobars at about twice the angle that they do over the sea. If the wind comes off the land from the right (as you stand facing the sea), the refraction effect and this 'gradient wind' effect are opposed and tend to cancel (Fig. 19.5a). However, if the wind comes off the land from the left the refraction and gradient wind effects are in the same direction, that is, the wind direction gets bent more seaward (Fig. 19.6a).

The bend in the wind as it breaks clear of the shore is not along the shore itself, but maybe takes place in the first mile or so of its passage over the sea and it depends on how the gradient wind is orientated to the shoreline whether the refraction effect will be enhanced or cancelled.

So whether there will be a bend in the wind as it crosses the coast or not depends on which side of the perpendicular to the coastline the wind comes from. With the wind behind you face the coastline. If the wind is from the left – little or no effect. If from the right hand – a shift of some $15°$ which is more seaward facing the sea but away from the perpendicular when facing

Figure 19.4 *(a) The off-shore wind 'toboggans' more directly off the coastline.*
(b) The similar thing for an on-shore wind.
(c) With an oblique wind direction some tobogganning occurs, but also allow for the wind being steered along a steep coastline.
(d) Neither of these effects will be much in evidence with a wind that is directed almost perpendicular to the shoreline

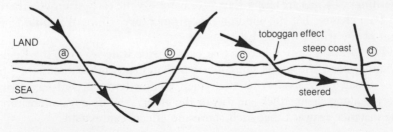

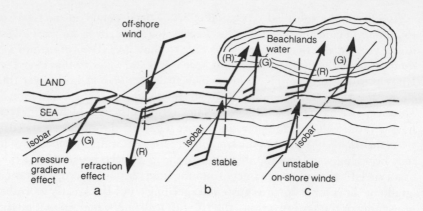

Figure 19.5 *(a) With an off-shore wind the lower friction of the sea bends the wind more towards the isobar (gradient wind) direction (G). When the wind is from the left facing the sea, the refraction effect (R) is opposed to (G) and over inshore waters the two tend to cancel. (b) With an on-shore wind a stable airstream will bend due to the gradient effect more than it will with (c) an unstable airstream; here the opposing refraction effect again tends to cancel out the gradient effect*

the land. (In the SH these rules will be reversed. The refraction effect is universal but the gradient effect is opposite in the SH.)

When winds blow at relatively small angles to a shoreline they tend to be steered along the shore. This applies to channels that have winds blowing slightly across them. If you have a channel that lies north-south and the wind is SSW or even SW, then in the channel it will be more nearly southerly. This is the 'steering' effect of even the most modest of shorelines. Give the coast some cliffs and the effect may literally extend miles offshore. For example *Royal Sovereign* light vessel is some eight miles south of Beachy Head where the cliffs that are the end of the Sussex Downs stand along the sea. The coast runs roughly northeast-southwest and so do the winds. At dawn 60 per cent of the winds are either from E/NE or W/SW and by the afternoon 60 per cent are from W/SW and a further 23 per cent from E/NE. That this is not a fluke result is confirmed when we find that at Dungeness some twenty miles further east, and although the coastline suddenly turns to the north, over 50 per cent of the winds on summer mornings (7 a.m.) are either E or W or calm. By the early afternoon there is an even chance that the wind on this promontory will be W, while 15 per cent of the winds will be E.

The message written here is that even a wide waterway like the English Channel steers the winds along it rather than in any other direction. Thus how much more likely is it that steep confined waters will have winds steered along them either one way or the other. And do not underestimate the distance seaward that such shoreside effects can extend.

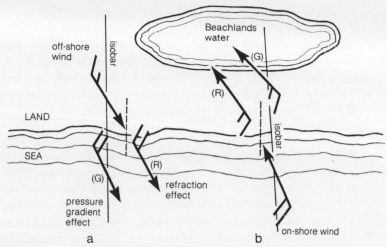

Figure 19.6 *The pressure gradient effect (G) and the refraction effect (R) will be in the same direction when:*
(a) an off-shore wind comes from the right (facing the sea) and (b) an on-shore wind comes from the right (facing the coast)

So to return to our inquiry into shoreside effects that might really amount to something. If the wind comes at an acute angle to the shoreline the toboggan effect may be there just along the shore, but the steering effect is the major one in a confined waterway (Fig. 19.4). On the other hand if the wind comes off the shore more directly, both the toboggan and the steering effects will be less marked.

The Effects of Promontories

On page 106 will be found the effects experienced in the lee of a monster promontory – the Rock of Gibraltar. Gibraltar may be a rather unique promontory, but the effects felt there will be reflected in the lee of any other bluff headland.

There are two major effects that need describing. The first is the 'lee eddy' effect where major rotating eddies produce gusty conditions and even winds that blow backwards against the trend of the wind (Fig. 19.7). These obviously occur most often and to the most marked degree when the headland is high and the slopes on the lee side are steep. Then 'falling' winds may be found on the lee side with wide variations in speed and direction.

The other effect is akin to the 'back-eddy' produced when the tidal stream or the flow of a river comes round a bend and takes the outside of the bend. The water on the inside of the bend can often be found going against the direction of the stream. Similarly, when a wind blows across the end of a headland that is relatively high there will be a rotating eddy in the lee of the headland but air, being a less well-behaved fluid than water, will not eddy in

103

nice predictable ways and many odd gusts and lulls will be induced closely under the steep slopes.

Elsewhere we also mention that major promontories that stand out in the path of the prevailing winds can have a marked effect in sheltering the bays beyond them. In this more sheltered environment seabreezes and other local winds can develop while elsewhere the strength of the prevailing wind may make them weak or impossible.

High Coasts

A coast where the foothills of the mountains, or sometimes the mountains themselves, rise out of the sea is always potentially dangerous. This is because of falling winds that are produced in several different ways. Heavy rain drags down air through which it falls and this air spreads out when it meets the surface. Air brought down in this way is usually a good deal colder than its surroundings and it thrusts out from the seat of the deluge as a cold squall. Being cold and dense the outflow from thunderstorms on mountain slopes that look on to the sea comes rushing down the inclines, particularly following the valleys, and emerges over inshore waters with the ferocity of a gale. As the previous weather has been hot the impact of this cold squall can be catastrophic. In place of light winds and topless temperatures you will need the protection of sweaters and buoyancy jackets especially as the unprepared will have taken a capsize.

It is important in this and any other venue to allow for the effects that thunderstorms can bring. If storms are forecast, or you can already hear thunder in the distance before you set sail, damn the inconvenience and take some protective clothing with you. If you are board sailing and intend to go

Figure 19.7 *The effects in the lee of elevated headlands include falling winds and lee eddies*

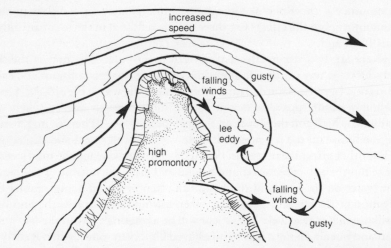

well away from 'home' then brave the comments and go out prepared for temperatures 10–15°F (5–8°C) lower than they are now and for the cold deluge of rain and/or hail that could come your way. If you are not too experienced be sensible and stay around your own bit of beach so that you can get ashore before any squalls hit you.

Not all falling winds are due to thunderstorms or heavy showers over slopes inland. Hefty mountains whose tops will be snow-covered, or close to it, generate great falling winds which are outsize katabatic winds. These may not be accompanied by any form of precipitation and in some cases the gale-force mountain blow can be under clear skies or perhaps dotted with cumulus clouds.

The best known of these winds is the mistral of the Gulf of Lions. The special conditions around the Gulf of Lions contribute to this great falling wind that is partly thermal in origin and partly large-scale. If the isobars over the Massif Central and the Alps are for wind from some point north, mistral is on the cards, because the mountains bottle up the air streaming from central Europe. Eventually, just as if it has been dammed, it bursts over through the available gaps and the major ones for mistral are the Garonne gap and Rhône valley. The mistral rises to its strongest over the *Inshore* waters at the mouth of the Rhône, but all the developing sailing areas between there and the Spanish border are very subject to it. If you sail this coast then mistral will be an ever-present threat to be considered. There are no months when the mistral is missing and it blows Force 6 on an average of four days even in its minimum months of September/October. In June/July there are an average of nine days a month with Force 6 mistral, four days with Force 7 and two days with Force 8. Only in the months of October/November does Force 8 hardly ever occur. In almost all months of the year there are one or two days when mistral blows everywhere along the coast between Spain and the Gulf of Genoa.

The orientation of the isobars, plus the cold dry air falling down the mountain slopes to the sea, make the wind reach its most vicious along the Gulf of Lions coasts, but that does not mean that there are not similar winds elsewhere. If there are mountains not very far inland and the general wind direction is given or forecast to be from over them, allow for falling winds and remember that valleys that look down onto the sea will aid the wind speed and make for eddies and turbulence where this enhanced river of wind meets bluff promontories or in some other way is thwarted on its way to the open sea. Even hills that will never qualify in anybody's book as mountains can add their impetus to wind, already strong, that blows over them, and if there are cliffs or high steep-to shores then what might have been Force 4–5 becomes Force 5–6 or more and Force 6–7 becomes 7–8.

Forecasts will never allow for such effects and winds forecast or actually blowing from shorewards, which have a real bit of strength behind them must be treated with considerable care when sailing *Inshore* waters.

Recently during a holiday I went out on the long peninsula that sticks out into the Irish Sea from Wales and is called the Lleyn Peninsula. There are three big bluff mountains called The Rivals on the west coast and we had stopped downwind of them. The day was overcast with much low stratus cloud that was coming in on the SW wind. It was truly maritime Tropical air and the clouds sat like caps over the tops of the three hills. Then a curious thing happened. Two streams of cloud came towards us from different directions, one round the high promontory from the southwest, the other directed down a valley from the southeast. The two streams met and created aerial whirlpools in the region where they clashed. I personally have never seen anything like it, but I suspect that it is a fairly normal occurrence in mountainous regions where the wind can be deflected by the height of the local topography. With such rotating and converging winds so relatively close above the surface, it would not be surprising if echoes of that confrontation above did not find their way into the surface wind. Here is another example of what may happen on high coasts or in hilly or mountainous terrain when the winds come from certain quarters.

A good example of the remarkable effect that high promontories may have on the wind in their lee is illustrated by what happens at Gibraltar when the wind blows over the Rock. Dangerous eddies form behind the Rock and extend some one or two miles downwind in a corridor about a mile wide. With easterly winds the danger zone extends over the whole of Gibraltar Harbour and when sailing dinghies or boards in the lee of high coasts, where single eminences rise proud above the rest of the surrounding land, it is as well to allow for such eddies. Local people will know if such turbulence occurs and under what circumstances, but if you do not ask you may not be told.

The windsurfers are getting into more and more exotic places – places which might never see a conventional dinghy – and as I am writing this I have been fascinated by an article in an American magazine about sailing a desert lake not far from Las Vegas where the temperature habitually goes to over 110°F (43°C). The naked lava stoops down to the dark blue water and the hot desert squalls blast in at 40 knots. There are dust storms to be contended with and a real seasonal change in wind speed, with autumn producing next-to-no-wind on most occasions – but not all. When fronts traverse the area then winds can go from light to full gale in a very short space of time.

This is just an example of how a sailing craft that you can strap onto any roof-rack is destined to go where perhaps no man has gone before. When, as an adventurous sailboarder, you make for watery pastures new, whatever you may find out about the local conditions could be quite inadequate because no one has ever needed to know about the tricks of the wind in such localities in the detailed way that you do. So take the adventure gently.

Rollers in the Wind

The airflow in the lee of hills and mountains can be very strange and may extend miles from the ridge that stands athwart the wind. The waves generated by the Snowdon range in Wales are beautifully illustrated in photographs and are at some twenty miles' distance from the main ridge. Each lens-shaped cloud (altocumulus lenticularis) is a visible sign of a whale-back of rising air that will soon cool and sink only to warm and rise again further on. This 'wave streaming' can on occasions produce rotating cylinders of air which will reverse the wind direction under them. These may be tens of miles from the ridges and so be over an area of sea which the faraway hills would seem to be quite incapable of affecting.

Wave streaming with or without rollers (and the latter are relatively uncommon) can be recognised by lens-shaped clouds formed at any altitude. They will have a curious property which is well known in hilly districts but is rare over the flatlands, and that is the ability to remain stationary. This follows because the waves set up in the airstream are the only reason for the clouds being there. Air streams uphill towards the crest of a wave and in so doing condenses its water-vapour into cloud. As the air runs downhill beyond the wave crest it warms and evaporates the cloud away. Thus the clouds stay where the waves are.

The position of waves and rollers will change with time because the condition of the airstream changes with time. Late afternoon and evening will see the correct conditions more than the middle of the day and such wave clouds also grow dense in advance of coming fronts. It is likely that a roller will reveal its presence by a larger than normal (and darker than normal) cumulus cloud which again appears to remain in one place. However, if you are under the roller the cloud will be above you and will look dark and strangely woolly in texture. There may also be a 'helm bar' on the ridge or mountain from which the wind comes. This helm, the rollers and the lenticular clouds are shown in Fig. 19.8.

Figure 19.8 *Features of clouds and winds formed in a stable, moist airstream downwind of a hill ridge. There may sometimes be retrograde winds immediately in the lee of the ridge as well as rollers further away*

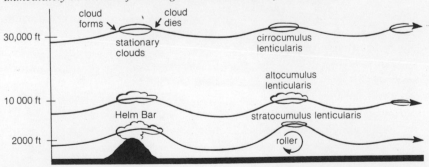

The effects of wave streaming are felt a great distance from the ridges that create them, but when sailing close under high ground that looks down into the water you may experience standing eddy streaming. Here you will be very surprised to find that the wind is consistently towards the high ground despite the fact that you know the isobars are for wind from over the hills and clouds sailing by above confirm it. However, such contrary wind can appear in an otherwise cloudless airstream and seem to be quite inexplicable until you realise that the flow is just like that in lee of any solid barrier.

Before we leave the realm of those who sail off the beach onto the open sea I must reiterate the warning to board sailors to take extreme care when the wind is blowing from the shore. Lose your board in these conditions and you will see it drift rapidly out to sea. You, not wishing to lose so much valuable merchandise, could struggle after but you will not make it. If that happens and the shore is not far then make for the shore or attract the attention of local craft. Let someone else bring your board back – you just stay afloat.

20 Beachland Sailing

Because you are not far from the main sea coast, but are largely protected from sea and swell, so wave tactics are less important in this venue. You can also hope to start off dry and end up drier than you would be when chucking-up the spray from waves that slap against the bow as you beat or reach to windward. For the relative newcomer this is much safer sailing because it is remarkable how even quite a short traverse over land cuts the wind speed. However, if you intend to sail across a harbour or estuary mouth when the wind is blowing with some force straight off the sea there is more potential danger here than on the open ocean. For one thing constraining the wind to blow within narrower confines speeds it up in harbour entrances (or in arms of the sea that look directly into the wind that is blowing) and if the tide is ebbing against the blow then the wind-against-tide chop can get so short and steep as to have you capsized in a mass of white water. That can be a dangerous situation and in these circumstances you must never leave the buoyancy of the boat as the rescue services struggle to organise and bring you back into quiet water against an ebb that is carrying you rapidly seaward.

It seems like a miraculous change when the tide slackens and turns even though the wind has not changed appreciably. Now what was all white horses and a very difficult, lumpy passage transforms into a much more manageable simple seaway.

It is of all land venues the beachlands that will feel seabreeze effects if they are going to occur at all. Calm, bright mornings can have the seabreeze drifting in as early as breakfast-time, but you have (as outlined on page 110) to note the wind direction and speed to make sensible predictions of what will happen in other circumstances. In any case you have to remember that a calm morning may only be calm because the overnight inversion layer is locking the true wind away aloft and as soon as the sun gets to work on the land that upstairs wind will be down on the surface and it will no longer be calm. Here it helps to have listened to a forecast – or to have looked at one on the TV – and to have noted the general direction of the isobars. Sometimes they just say 'light, variable with seabreezes on coasts' which once again leaves you on your own.

Measurements made on the South Coast of England at Thorney Island, which is set between arms of the sea and is 3 miles (5 km) in from the main sea coast, show that when the wind at breakfast-time is less than 10 knots there is possibility of seabreeze setting in before the afternoon is out. The less the wind (which has to be blowing from landward) the earlier will the calm (that preceeds the breeze) begin to show. So in this venue it may start off almost calm in the early morning followed by some wind as the sun breaks the inversion. This wind will be temporarily replaced by another calm as the seabreeze builds against the off-shore wind.

The nearer the Equator you sail the more likely it is that seabreeze will be able to pull in against stronger winds than Force 3. On the Mediterranean Coast of North Africa the seabreeze habitually blows at 25 knots and so theoretically can stop and reverse an off-shore 25-knot morning wind. Most places in the Mediterranean and similar will have seabreeze regimes that can bring in the breeze against winds of Force 4 (11–16 knots) or even Force 5 (17–21 knots). To return to Britain and latitudes close to hers, it is unusual for a morning wind of 10 knots from the land to allow a seabreeze to actually reverse the off-shore wind. However, the seabreeze force, acting against the wind that exists, may well cut the wind speed in the middle of the day and in other circumstances winds of Force 4 or more (which have components along the main coastline) can be bent by the seabreeze. You can think of the direction as a bi-metallic strip which will be bent towards inland as the temperature increases and to which the force applied grows with the day and wanes again with evening so that it relaxes back to its original direction as the sun sinks. We can consider the rigidity of the strip itself to increase with wind speed (Fig. 20.1) and so the shift in wind direction on a day of strong wind is less marked.

How to make up your mind as to when a breeze is about to arrive is covered on pages 112–113 and it is rather complicated because the further you are inland the later will be the breeze. At first the seabreeze will appear

Figure 20.1 *The bi-metallic strip analogy to the thermal bending that occurs on good seabreeze days, but where the wind is too strong to result in a true breeze. In a bi-metallic strip the outer (dark) metal expands more than the inner and so bends the strip as the temperature increases*

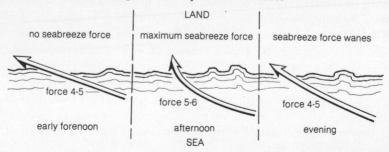

LAND

no seabreeze force | maximum seabreeze force | seabreeze force wanes

force 4-5

force 5-6

force 4-5

early forenoon | afternoon | evening

SEA

along the main sea coast (or in indentations of that coast) and later will march inland behind a seabreeze front rolling back the previously off-shore wind. I have defined the *Beachland* region with this in mind. It often takes a couple of hours for the breeze to travel three miles (5 kilometres) inland, but that means that most *Beachland* venues will have the breeze by lunch-time, if they are to get it at all. On odd occasions a battle develops between the seabreeze and the off-shore wind which is fairly evenly matched and then sudden – and often short-lived – periods of seabreeze appear late in the afternoon, causing remarkable reversals of tactical positions as what was windward becomes leeward and vice versa. It certainly pays to have some idea in your mind that these breezes can occur and at roughly what period of the day they may occur so that you can look out for them and not suddenly be caught in a wind reversal for which you can see no reason and whose behaviour you cannot understand.

Late in the afternoon you have to be ready for the wind off the land to come back and sweep the seabreeze away. This happens sometimes as the sun loses its power and the off-shore wind, that has been thwarted all day, pounces on the faltering breeze and overcomes it. Also when showers or thunderstorms build up in the middle of the day or during the afternoon and a seabreeze is blowing, it is prudent to expect sudden gusts and related wind shifts because the downdraughts out of the cumulonimbus clouds pour wind onto the surface like water and this can beat the seabreeze. Such downdraught winds stem from the storm centres themselves which gives an idea of from where the squalls may come. The effect of each storm usually lasts something like half an hour and then the seabreeze may come back for a while only to be swept away again by the next storm.

Recognising Seabreeze Shifts

The wind shift when a seabreeze front passes may be sudden or take place over an extended period. The sharpest changes come with winds that can be seen to be full of convection currents by virtue of the heap (cumulus) clouds they grow. While cumulus can grow in winds from any direction there is no doubt that in temperate latitudes it is the NW wind which is the most likely to be unstable and grow heap clouds. It is not the clouds themselves which aid the seabreeze penetration, but the generally unhindered up-currents that made them. This follows because the seabreeze front is a sort of linear chimney up which the wind from the land and the opposing breeze from the sea must ascend. So a day which is already primed for up-currents is the most likely one to have a quick-moving seabreeze front and thus a rapid shift of wind direction as it crosses you.

When Will I Get the Seabreeze?

In the *Beachland* venue you are sometimes too near to the main sea coast to be able to recognise where the seabreeze wind shift is by virtue of the seabreeze front. The latter has often not had time to really organise in the first few miles and so the line of darker cumulus stretched parallel to the coast that shows where the up-currents are strongest (and so where the surface calm patch is) may not be very evident. However, I have seen the front marked by a meagre line of the only cloud in the sky and that was quite near the South Devon coast so one cannot be dogmatic about it for all occasions.

Having made up your mind that a seabreeze is likely (that is, there is more sunshine than cloud and the wind is less than 10 knots from landward or perhaps parallel to the coast itself), you then have to keep an eye towards seaward to try and detect its coming. It will help to have an idea of roughly what period of the day the breeze usually puts in an appearance and that depends on the opposing wind speed. We can best illustrate this by a

Figure 20.2 *Seabreeze clock for Beachland and Coastland venues. (This diagram first appeared in* Wind Pilot.)

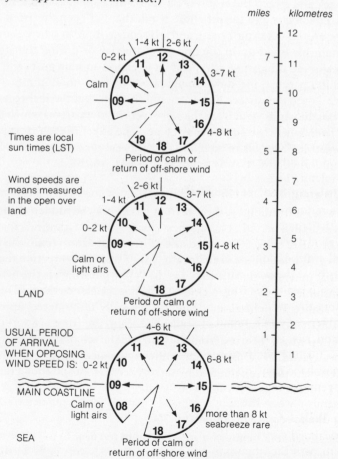

diagram I first used in *Wind Pilot* which I have called the Seabreeze Clock (Fig. 20.2). The diagram is, I think, self-explanatory once you have looked into it and asked yourself questions such as:

If I am sailing a couple of miles inland from the main sea coast and the wind around 9 a.m. is, I estimate, about 4 knots, when can I expect a seabreeze?

The answer is 'Somewhere around 11 a.m. local sun time (LST)'. You cannot be absolutely sure of when it will arrive, but at least you will not expect it before 10 a.m. and if it has not arrived by 2 p.m. there must be a good reason why.

So the morning wind speed and the seabreeze clock give you some idea of when the breeze might arrive. The exact moment of its arrival is something you can only divine on the spot and here are some pointers:

i the immediate sign of onset is a calming wind,
ii craft further to seaward may be already becalmed or be sailing in an on-shore breeze,
iii the front often builds a line of denser, darker cumulus cloud along it and the shift should be somewhere under that line,
iv the soaring birds such as swallows, swifts, gulls etc. use the updraughts feeding the front and an unusual number of them may help you identify the front on a day with little cloud.

On days with clear air and good visibility the front travels fast and clears across you quickly, but on hazy over-warm days it may be very sluggish. Then the calm zone under the front takes many minutes to clear and on such days, even though it is so hot, the front may get no further than three or four miles inland. This is because the heat is induced by a subsidence inversion near the ground which inhibits the upward currents which must exist if the seabreeze and the opposing off-shore wind are to escape as they collide along the front.

On good days the breeze moves in behind its front at some 1½–2 knots, but it itself will be blowing at three or four times that speed. This would be impossible if the extra wind speed could not ascend into the seabreeze front. Days with air masses in which convection currents occur naturally are therefore the ones which allow the breeze to go racing inland and end up several tens of miles inland by the end of the afternoon. They are the ones where on, say, a south-facing coast a NW morning wind is suddenly shifted to S so turning windward into leeward and vice versa.

If you have done your homework and are expecting a breeze then the above remarks can help you make up your mind how important it is to hug the shallows when the tide is adverse. A run that becomes a beat (or vice versa) due to seabreeze action and does it in a minute or so does not leave you becalmed very long, but if the calm zone is going to take ten minutes or more to pass then being in the worst of the stream could be disastrous.

Conversely, with a favourable tidal set towards the sea and the prospect of a long period of calm you would be better off in the stream as it will carry you through to where the seabreeze is blowing. However, if the stream is directed away from the coast – which is the way the seabreeze calm zone is moving – you could be trapped in a constant calm as you and calm zone move inland together.

Clubs near the entrances to harbours and estuaries, which send their fleets to turning marks lying up inland-going creeks or rivers on seabreeze mornings, may be subjecting them to a very frustrating sail as they struggle to make it through the calms under the seabreeze front. If the front has already passed them it will be a run and as the calm zone only moves in at about 2 knots the leaders will run into the calm and so become trapped there. Everyone else with more breeze to drive them on will come up behind and the whole fleet will lie in a huddle of colliding booms and frantic shouts for water. They will stay locked to the edge of the calm zone as firmly as if held by a rope. Only as *it* decides to move can they move.

If the front has not yet passed, the passage up the creek will be some form of a beat or close reach. With adverse ebbing tide and a light off-shore wind the front could conceivably overtake the fleet from the back leaving the leaders even further ahead. Or they could all make it round the turning mark at the head of a channel or creek and then be running back when the leaders strike the calm zone. If that calm does not pass quickly all the tail-end-charlies run down and catch the leaders. The new leaders are those who manage to work their way into the seabreeze and set off beating back down the channel. It is worth noting that almost invariably the seabreeze is stronger than the opposing wind so craft that get into the breeze first get a great advantage.

There will obviously be all kinds of different situations brought about by the passage of the seabreeze calm zone across the fleet during a race and only understanding of the way it all works can provide useful practical answers to what to do when it comes to sailing through the actual conditions. Do not forget that once the breeze is in it usually stays in and blows steadily.

There is one other useful pointer to the coming breeze and that is brought about by the sinking air to seaward of the seabreeze front. The descending air stops convection and so the cloud over the inshore waters and the coast itself disappears to leave absolutely total sunshine. On the inland side of the front, convection still goes on and sometimes local cloud cover becomes temporarily almost total. Thus when it is quite cloudy where you are and brilliant conditions can be seen towards the coast you know you have a seabreeze wind shift coming. Further, the air from the sea is clear and cool whereas that from over the land is usually hazy. The clear sunshine viewed through this haze is a characteristic of a coming seabreeze which once seen and understood for what it is will not easily be forgotten.

You can often identify those clouds which are part of the seabreeze front by the cloud 'curtains' that hang wisp-like below them. There are stronger updraughts into these clouds than into normal cumulus and it is not unknown for the seabreeze front to become a line of showers that have in them the seeds of their own destruction as the downdraught produced by the falling rain acts against, and sometimes kills, the updraught. If the latter cannot occur the seabreeze fails to make it inland and may even be swept back out to sea.

There are days when the wind speed off the land is just too strong for the breeze to get any further than the beach. A warmed beach is the first chance the newly formed breeze has to acquire convection currents and until it can escape upwards its speed is very slight. So once the edge of the seabreeze carpet is over the beach in comes the breeze and up go the convection clouds to shade the beach and so reduce the breeze. The off-shore wind can then win and it pushes the clouds out over the sea. The sun comes out on the beach and the whole thing repeats. It leads to very erratic wind shifts close inshore and it can also occur when the front has got further inland.

21 The Day's Wind

The way the wind varies depends on how convection currents can grow in it or on the degree of inversion 'lid' it has acquired. Whenever cloud clears during the day the lumpiness of the wind will increase and we must not forget the rule that a lumpy sky means a lumpy wind to go with it. Thus overcast mornings (or even whole days) indicate a wind that flows pretty smoothly and only acquires variations due to hitting obstacles upwind. A coastwise wind off the sea under these conditions will blow very smoothly, but it will get turbulent eddies in it once it gets ashore. You cannot use these eddies in any tactical way. You just find your way through them as best you can.

When a cloud layer begins to be 'burned off' by the sun then after a while variability begins to build in the wind. The wind speed will probably increase too but it is the direction shifts that are important in tactical sailing and these can be substantial. It has been proved statistically that over the land the morning period is the most variable of the day. The afternoon wind may be stronger, but it is less variable than the morning wind.

If the wind is too strong for seabreeze effects to make much of an impression on it then the wind will go through its diurnal variation (page 53) increasing in speed into the afternoon and then decreasing with evening. As the sun sinks so does the speed and in fact we can say that normally the wind speed follows the sun, being greatest when the sun is highest and going down as the sun sinks. There are however some details to be added here.

As soon as the earth cools below the temperature of the air the convection currents that were present earlier become cut off. This immediately cuts the variations in the wind and it begins to lose any tactical variability it had earlier. There may be shifts in the wind during evening races, but no one will be able to divine what they are in advance.

Also, as the evening progresses even quite reasonable winds begin to become unreliable and desert you for periods – often, it seems, just when a strong tidal stream is getting you into dangerous proximity with a buoy or moored boat. These 'holes' in the wind are characteristic of evening and it is never wise to rely on an evening wind. There is very often a calm or very light period after dark which is followed by a noctural wind from the land towards midnight.

By day if cloud cover cuts off the sun which has previously been bright then again the convection currents will be inhibited and variability will become disorganised as well as normally becoming less as the sun disappears. An example is when the high cloud ahead of a coming warm front or occlusion streams in above. The weather is usually very pleasant at these times and the wind is not usually much more than Force 3–4. Its direction is often around west and attractive lumps of cotton-wool cloud populate the sky.

However, once the cloud begins to cut the sun from the land these well-rounded lumps start to become grey and fragmented. When that happens you can say goodbye to reliable gusts and lulls with their attendant shifts. The wind will not blow smoothly – it will still have variations in it – but the gust cells are not being formed like they were before and rhyme and reason may well go out of the wind at the same time.

The temperature inversion that forms over the land during the night has to be broken in the morning and it is convection currents that do it. However, in the early part of the day the inversion may act like a sort of elastic membrane spread over the surface air. The bubbles of the thermals may lift and try to break the membrane but they cannot, and while there are up and down currents these are quite small in vertical extent.

It is often under these conditions that abnormally variable winds may occur and with such winds the speed will not be great. In fact it is a rule that only light to moderate winds can possibly have wide variations in their direction. Thus the very variable morning wind is a perfect candidate to be replaced by a seabreeze and then we get one of the most dramatic changes in wind type you could expect.

The seabreeze is usually a wind with very little variability. It blows from seaward and that is it. Thus all of a sudden in the late morning there will be a complete change of wind type from perhaps the most variable of daytime winds blowing from landward to the least variable blowing from seaward. We see an example of this in Fig. 21.1. The morning wind was generally NE, but was so light up to 8 a.m. that the pen arm of the speed recorder

Figure 21.1 *The normal way a seabreeze sets in against an off-shore wind at a site which is 3 miles (5 km) inland from the main sea coast*

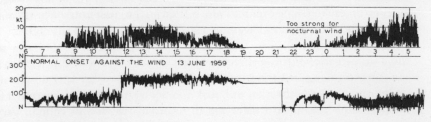

would not actuate. Then the speed trace showed behaviour that goes with abnormally variable winds. There are gaps of some minutes in the trace showing almost calm or very little wind.

However, it is the direction trace that commands attention. At 6.30 a.m. the wind was close to N and then it went slowly through some 60° to ENE. It took nearly an hour to complete that shift! The following shifts are not quite so long, but you will see how the wind shifts in little steps through very wide angles as one bit of wind-field replaces the other. At one time between about 10.30 a.m. and 11.15 a.m. the wind shifted in this manner through a full 80° before coming back through about 50–60°. These are incredibly big shifts, but they are not at all unique and when winds blow from landward under inversion layers they are very prevalent.

Yet none of these shifts was as big as the one when the seabreeze suddenly came in and the wind shifted from NE to beyond S – a shift of some 160°. After which the seabreeze was in for the afternoon. Note that while you could have expected a backing phase of the morning wind to follow a veering phase and to have in the main been right, there is no such predictability about any shifts that occur in the seabreeze. There are a few variations, but they are short-lived and on the whole for most of the afternoon the wind just blew from about 200° getting to its strongest around mid-afternoon and then sinking into obscurity by 5 p.m. In fact, as so often happens after seabreeze days, the wind dies completely for over two hours and two hours is a long time when you have been 'down channel' and need to get back against the ebb. Only rescue boats or handy passing cruisers are likely to help on these occasions which are the rule rather than the exception. If you get a seabreeze day make plans for no wind after tea-time.

Much later, when all normal dinghy and board sailors are in the bar or in bed, the night wind began to blow and was a very different wind from the one of the previous morning. The direction was the same, but the variations had gone out of it which is what we expect at night. However, the speed grew markedly and without help from convection currents (which are the agents that increase the wind by day) this must have been due to the isobars tightening and so increasing the gradient wind. It grew to a very variable 8–10 knots next day with gusts and lulls swinging widely from 20 knots to nothing. It also stuck rigidly to the NE while the seabreeze forces fought all day to overcome it. Eventually at 3.30 p.m. the seabreeze won and another 160° sudden shift occurred. Then, despite the relative strength of the wind before the breeze the same evening calm settled on the coast until once again the night wind blew now and again at a strength of a few knots throughout the night.

This sudden shift of the seabreeze, whenever it occurs, is characteristic when it has set in against the wind, but it is as well to realise that on very calm mornings the seabreeze will just wander slowly and often rather erratically from a landward direction to its usual seaward direction. Or when the morning wind is stronger and some bigger than normal cumulus clouds build over the land the seabreeze may come in for an hour or two and then be swept away by the killing effects of showers which will be most likely in the afternoon. At other times a wild and capricious shift system occurs with the seabreeze forces pulling the wind from a shoreward point towards seaward only to find its impetus broken by the cold downdraughts from a hefty shower or thunderstorm. This produces wild swings in direction – in some cases from say E through N to S and back to N, the whole impossible phase lasting perhaps a couple of hours before one or other of the combatants wins and the wind either stays back off the land where it was before, or the sun comes out and the seabreeze is in for the rest of the day.

All these things and more can happen and not every one can be explained or even recognised. Most of the time the wind will act in the ways we are describing as being normal, but there are other times when it is impossible to give a convincing reason why the wind did what it did. However, just because a percentage of the time you do not know what is happening, that is no reason for not trying to understand all other occasions when things are going according to the rules.

22 Thermals Along the Shore

The earth's surface is a patchwork of different abilities to warm up under the sun's rays. Those parts which are solid and flat warm up most while those that filter and absorb the rays in depth warm up least. A good example is an airfield. The runways heat up well above the surrounding grassland and become centres for the formation of thermals. An allied example is a road surrounded by arable crops. Whenever we see the mirage effect of 'water on the road' it is evidence that the road surface is very warm and is a potential thermal source. However, runways and roads may not produce as many thermals as might be expected because the slipstream of aircraft or cars will break up the developing thermals. Better surfaces may be hillsides facing the direct sun and it is over such slopes that glider pilots seek their thermal lift. Ploughed or well-cropped grassland surrounded by woods will act as sources of thermals and a constant succession of them will be produced from such areas to form cloud streets down the wind.

Near the water any shore is a potential thermal source and when mud-flats glint in the sun they can be expected to be places towards which air will drift when there is absolute flat calm and you are looking for any zephyr you can find. However, it is also a fact that patches of water can have very different temperatures and over the warmer water air will rise so that a local drift will occur from the cooler to the warmer patches. As you have no means of telling where such patches exist all that can be said is that in flat-calm conditions the perturbing fact that other craft seem to have a bit of wind that you do not have, need not mean that Lady Luck is smiling on them and not on you – it could just be that they happen to be along a line of division between one water temperature and another.

I once won a race at Dell Quay at the top of Chichester Harbour with the aid of such a one. Because it dries at low water the regatta had to be staged on a day with high water around the end of the afternoon when the classes were coming home to finish. It was a hot day and there was not much wind. In fact, as we struggled up the arm of the sea at whose head lay the finish, it became less and less. Luckily it was also top of the tide or none of us would have made it. It was also the time when the shore water would have been very warm and the incoming tidal water cooler, so that a real contrast between the water in the middle and at the edges of the creek could have become established. There were several of us in the leading gaggle, but we were more in the middle of the creek braving the possibility that the tide had turned. The others were hugging the shores. Amazingly, as it seemed, we and we alone fell in with a little private wind that added to the slight wind everyone else had and which carried us lonely as a cloud out ahead of the rest round the turning mark and so back to finish well ahead of the next boat. At the time I could not think what had happened. Now I believe that we were the happy recipients of a thermally-induced breeze set up between the cool water we were in and the warm shoreside water. Another example of this effect will be found on page 91 (the 'phantom beach' effect).

It helps to be able to visualise invisible thermals and research has shown that they look very much like vast bubbles of warming air swelling up over a source area when they are first initiated. They must look something like a hot-air balloon at lift-off. The thermal bubble may be perhaps 50–100 yards (metres) across and its difference in temperature above its surroundings need only be a degree or two. Yet it gathers and thrusts off from the surface and if you could see it, it would look very like a vast jellyfish as it pulses itself upwards into the air. The jellyfish analogy is apt because the nastier kinds of jellyfish have long trailing tentacles and these give an impression of the wake of the thermal as its lifts higher (Fig. 22.1). The warm air rises in the middle and as it cools rolls over at the top and sinks down the outside.

Dinghies and boards have a chance to feel the effects of thermals because a beach or mud-flat in the sun is bound to be hotter than the water that laps it. Thus the temperature contrast exists close to the shore and as the thermals lift off there is air motion into the space where the thermal was. This must come off the water onto the shore and so the edge in the sun is the

Figure 22.1 *How thermals form and induce the formation of cumulus clouds:*
(a) a thermal bubble warms above its surroundings
(b) the bubble lifts off
(c) the thermal rises, expands and cools
(d) when it has cooled to dewpoint temperature cloud forms

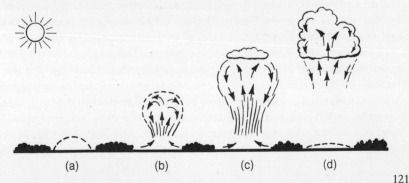

(a)   (b)   (c)   (d)

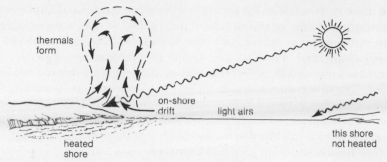

Figure 22.2 *Finding shoreside drift due to thermals*

place to be in those windless states when even steerage way deserts you (Fig. 22.2).

For example, you come round a turning mark on a narrow creek or river and it seems pretty equally divided as to which side to choose on the way back, but the sun is out and the wind is going down and down. Take the side away from the sun because flats or banks there will have become the warmest surfaces around. Pulses of useful air will occur along this shore and by sitting (or standing) stock still and canting the sails towards the shore, way can be induced which once established can carry you with the momentum gained from one brief pulse of air to the next and so keep you inching down the shore.

The idea is always given that thermals are entities that are more or less round in section and so must induce local brief zephyrs of wind after which there is a return to flat calm as the next thermal builds. However, my experience leads me to believe that shores in direct sunlight can induce a kind of linear thermal lift that produces a more-or-less continuous on-shore drift most of the way along the shore. One morning race I remember was down the sunny side of a south-going creek and we managed to escape the ruck of boats and get a little clear wind. Somehow we seemed to gain an early advantage just by sitting stock still, hardly daring to breathe and allowing gravity to put a flow into the sails. In this way we pulled clear so that by the time some of the rest were breaking out of everyone else's dirty wind we had escaped some fifty yards or more ahead of the next boat. That advantage came from the 'linear' thermal effect along a shore that was dried-out mud-flats with their rounded surfaces taking full force of the direct sunlight. Mud-flats can often be cambered like an aircraft's wing and just as smooth, and it is a rule of creek sailing that where the flat goes steep-to into the water there is going to be enough depth for at least partial plate. So as maximum thermal effect is to be found as close to the land-water division as possible, a nicely rounded mud shore is most likely to provide some early wind in flat-calm morning conditions. Another advantage of the mud-flats is that they are naturally carved and smoothed into contours that are conducive to laminar flow. Airflow may be laminar or turbulent but eddying, turbulent flow is the natural way for wind. Only when the air is moving slowly, is stable and the surface is smooth can anything approaching laminar (or layered) flow occur. We find it here under these early morning conditions and it sets in in the evenings when the inversion forms close to the ground. Once you have laminar flow you will not forget it, because of the unaccustomed steadiness of the wind and the lazy way that the minor shifts of direction wander slowly backwards and forwards. It is so easy to follow these shifts and the boat seems to have found at last the kind of airflow in which you feel it could be totally happy. Unfortunately, laminar flow is rarely experienced by day although cruising people will know it when they creep into or out of creeks or estuaries under cover of darkness using the sidling, slipping night wind that is finding its nocturnal way to the sea.

23 By the River Bank

The heading does not restrict this chapter to rivers because wherever you sail on small waters you are bound to get in the lee of trees, hedges, copses, buildings etc. However, it is in the narrow confines of rivers that you meet the most frustrating conditions – hence the title.

The way the shoreside objects alter the wind in their lee will depend on several things and these include:

i what kind of objects they are – lines of trees act in a different way from copses of them and copses act differently to buildings,
ii how high the objects are in general – and that often is an almost impossible thing to assess when the hampering obstacles have gaps in them,
iii how far you are from the obstacles – there are some interesting effects to be considered here,
iv whether the airstream is stable or unstable, that is, full of gusts,
v how fast the wind is blowing and from what direction compared to the run of the obstacles in its path.

With so many things to be considered it is inevitable that only a certain amount of guidance can be given, but you can learn a good deal on land before even going afloat. For instance, I was walking the dog up a stubble field the other day. The field had a hedge on the windward side and it was blowing about Force 4–5. I was watching the swallows gathering insects and was intrigued to see that none of them were flying close in along the hedge but further out. They seemed to have a constant patrol zone some way away from the hedge which indicated that it was there that the lowest wind speed was to be found and not up against the hedge itself. Insects cannot fly against strong winds and so will always seek the most sheltered spots where the wind speed is least.

Now I was not too surprised at this because when I looked at the hedge I could see through it and therefore the wind could filter through it too. When you can see through a hedge or a line of trees on a bank then the lowest wind speed is not up against the hedge, but 5 tree-heights (h) away from it. This comes about because there is as in Fig. 23.1:

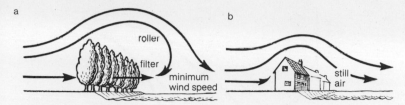

Figure 23.1 *(a) How lines of trees oppose the roller to the wind that filters through them which then produces minimum wind away from the trees (b) When air blows over a building or other solid barrier there is zero wind directly in lee*

i a roller in the lee of all obstructions,
ii a filter wind through obstructions with gaps in them.

The filter wind opposes the roller, making for more wind right up against the trees than where the two really get to grips which is the 5h from the trees mentioned above.

When there can be no filter wind as is the case with very dense masses of trees or as occurs in the lee of buildings, parapets, large craft that are moored or moving etc. then the wind will be zero right up against the dense obstruction and will gradually increase to become about 40 per cent of the unobstructed wind speed at the same 5h. However, with a medium-dense barrier that covers about half the windward space the wind speed at 5h is about half that which you would find in the lee of the building or other dense barrier, that is, it is about 20 per cent of the unobstructed wind speed (Fig. 23.2).

Thus it is the 5h zone of lowest wind speed that you will wish to avoid when sailing through the lee of barriers that possess a fairly even distribution of open spaces in them. I have always used a simple means of estimating this distance off and it is illustrated in Fig. 23.3. If the distance between the tips of thumb and forefinger when held at arm's length fit the height of the obstruction then you are five heights away from it. That is not the place to be. Either go further away or possibly come closer in and creep along the bank close up to the trees as is evident from Fig. 23.2.

How much further away? you may ask. For almost full wind speed, whatever barrier type is involved, you want to be thirty barrier heights away and you will be about 30h from a barrier when it fits into your thumbnail, again held at arm's length. However, you may not be able to get that far away. Houses are going to be some 30 feet high and fully-grown trees will be two or three times that height. As 30 feet is 10 yards (near enough 10 metres) so houses will affect the wind to a distance which is some 30 yards from them while a fully developed wood that rises out of the water's edge may affect the wind up to 100 yards from it.

Dense and open barriers allow almost full wind speed when you are

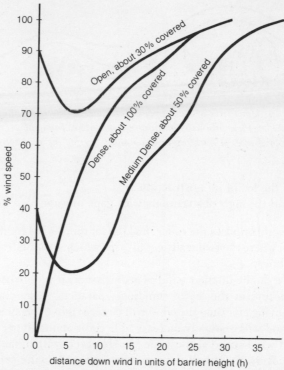

Figure 23.2 *The results of research into the wind speed downwind of barriers of different density. (Based on a figure in* Wind and Sailing Boats.*)*

twenty barrier heights away and this distance is again on your thumb being roughly the distance from tip to knuckle. It is the barrier which is half covered by trees and foliage that slows the wind most and at 20h you will in this case still not have much more than half the undisturbed wind speed.

Now how about the windward side of the obstruction? How far to windward of lee-shore obstructions does their effect extend? The answer is: out to about 10h, but on the windward side the minimum speed is found at 2h – usually too close to a medium dense barrier of trees to be of practical importance. So it is worth noting that at 5h to windward of open and dense barriers you will have about 80 per cent of the wind, but only some 60 per cent of the full strength when the barrier is truly medium dense (Fig. 23.4).

This gives the facts about barriers to the wind, but there are other things to be considered. The profile of the top of a dense wood that stoops down to the water's edge will affect what we have just been saying. If the shore is steep so that the air is guided down towards the water then maximum wind speed will be found closer in than you might otherwise think, but if the shore is flat and the wood comes cliff-like to the water's edge then it will act in much the same way as has been described above. The principle obviously

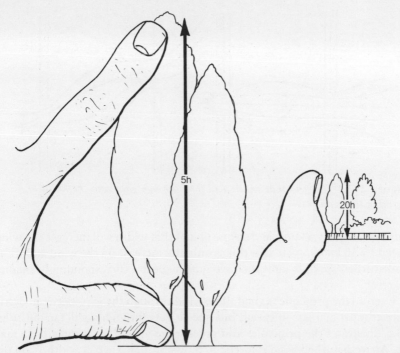

Figure 23.3 *The way to estimate where the zones of lowest wind speed and reasonable wind speed are to be found*

is that anything that tends to give the air a smooth passage over it will have less effect on the wind speed. It has been proved that five rows of trees slow the wind more than seven rows because the latter smooths the flow over them better and thus the inference is that where a wood, whose extent you cannot hope to gauge from the water, seems to go a fair way back from the water it will have a more orderly wind pattern in its lee than a narrower grove.

It is well known that the wind seeks the gaps in the shoreside obstructions and it is a rough rule that the size of gap × increase in speed tends to be constant. Thus a gap of a certain width may increase the wind speed

Figure 23.4 *The flow to windward of a barrier. Here the 5h yardstick of your thumb will tell you where the wind is still reasonable*

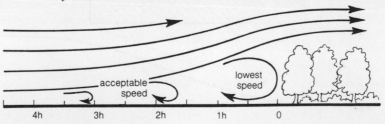

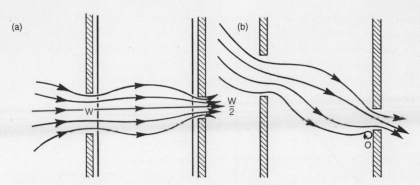

Figure 23.5 *The way that winds will flow through gaps and the kinds of patterns that can arise*

through it by say 5 knots and so one of half that width will increase the wind speed by 10 knots. Note that this is only the increase on the wind and if the undisturbed speed is light then we must expect a correspondingly smaller increase.

Even so the principle is good. The wind through the gaps between dense barrier must increase in speed, but once it gets through it will fan out. Fig. 23.5 illustrates the principles and gives some idea of what the effects may be. An undisturbed wind is forced to blow through a gap of width W on the windward side of the river. The degree of fanning is not great, but on the lee side it is forced to flow through a gap of half the width and the degree of funnelling is much greater.

So if there are narrow openings and the obstructions are big enough to really funnel or fan the wind expect the effects to be more marked and to extend further from the obstructions.

If you want to draw streamlines yourself the principle behind them is quite simple. Each streamline must be accounted for. For example if we

Figure 23.6 *With the wind at an angle to a barrier your best course is as shown in order to avoid the light air pocket off the corner removed from the wind*

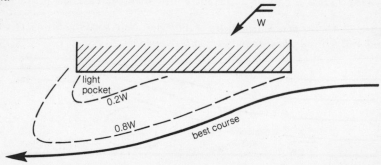

start off with five equally-spaced streamlines to represent the undisturbed wind we have to end up with five. However, they do not all have to go through the barriers because a line can be 'lost' by blowing over the barrier or it may be lost by useless collision with the obstructions in its path (O in Fig. 23.5b). Streamlines really embody the 'conservation of energy' principle – each streamline represents a part of the total energy of the wind and we can only lose that energy by friction or collision or by a streamline going out of the diagram to somewhere else, for example upwards over the top of the sails.

When the wind does not blow straight over a moderately dense barrier, but at an angle to it, it is found that the least wind is in a pocket under the end furthest from the wind. Thus if you have a gap between two barriers and a wind from over the quarter then you will get most wind close along the shore as the wind streams through the gap, but the best course to hold the wind is then as shown in Fig. 23.6. That is a gentle easing out from the bank to follow the 80 per cent of undisturbed wind speed as shown in the figure.

24 The Effect of Cliffs

When the wind blows off a cliff, or something resembling a cliff, there is bound to be a pocket of stagnant air in its lee. The problem is 'How far from the cliff-edge will the wind regain anything like its normal speed?' The answer to that depends on assessing how unstable the airstream is, because if there are plenty of vertically descending convection currents in it the wind is bound to become reasonable closer to the cliff than if the air is stable and is tending to flow in a layered (laminar) way.

Research and personal observation have proved to me that the distance at which the gusts will first get down on to the water is about 10h where h is the height of the cliff (Fig. 24.1). On our hand yardstick that is measured by the distance from thumb-tip to the joint of the thumb. If, when held at arm's length, that length just fits into the cliffs, then you are going to get help from gusts and inside the distance you will have much more chance of stagnant air. This follows because of the theory in Chapter 29, which shows that it is gusts from above barging into the daytime wind that speed up the latter.

However, the more lumpy the sky the more lumpy the wind and when big cumulus clouds build, the gusts may well come down closer to the cliff.

Figure 24.1 *The flow of wind off a cliff when the conditions are unstable. The wind becomes reasonable in speed at about 10h*

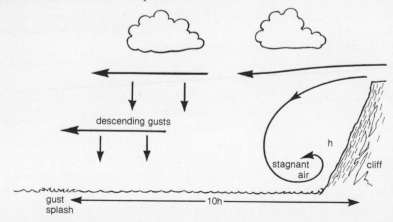

When showers come bursting over a high shoreline then falling winds will locally produce very strong gusts and squalls which should never be taken lightly (see 'Highland Sailing').

The above really applies to the inshore sailors and logically should have been included in that part. However, it fits naturally into this section as well if it is considered to be the maxi-end of a spectrum of solid barriers that tower at some height h above where you are sailing.

When sailing coastal creeks, particularly at low water, the sea walls etc. are possibly 20–30 feet (7–10 metres) above the water and thus 10h may be 100 yards (100 metres) away from the wall or whatever obstruction it is. As the wind speed may not be normal again before 20h–30h, it is evident that the wind may well be reduced right across a narrow creek, river etc. Villages that nestle by the water will of necesity have to be on rising ground so that at the highest springs or when there is a tidal surge they will not suffer flooding. They will consist of houses, boatyards, trees etc. and can well have an effective height above the water of 100 feet. Now 10h is to be found some 300 yards (300 metres) away and that may well be on the far mud-flats at low water meaning that the whole of the water channel running past the village is sheltered.

That is good, you may say, as it enables us to get afloat from the village hards without too much hassle. It also has its drawbacks because when a piece of water is sheltered then the contrast between the quiet surface wind periods and the sudden catastrophic gusts is vastly more marked than on the open water. As the trots and places where they moor are bound to be chock-a-block with craft then dinghies and boards will sail as close as they dare to the obstructions to sea room. When the stream is running fast, either flowing or ebbing, the desire to make as much along the available edges becomes paramount so that the danger of capsizing under a moored boat becomes increasingly likely. Having almost done it once or twice you get an idea of the horrors of being keel-hauled.

It is important to note that the villages and towns that stand on harbours and creeks have grown up where they are just because they were the most sheltered spots. People hate living in constant wind and will therefore have sited their houses in the lee of what higher ground there is. Thus it is very likely that you will get afloat where there is a considerable lee. You need to assess what the wind will be when you are clear of this shoreside hamper and the only way to do that is to sample the wind in the most open spot you can find. You can use an anemometer or just rely on your experience of what the wind on your cheek feels like when it is blowing a bit too much for comfort.

It is important in boats that can reef to put the reef in before you leave the shelter and so you need to know what to expect. If you have no other criterion then double the wind speed you have in the sheltered anchorages and act accordingly. Of course I know that no one puts in more reef than they need and usually it is rather less. However, when the wind is on the edge of what is curtains for your class it is often the well-reefed boat, or the boat with mainsail only, and who has thereby survived the capsizes, that makes it home to a place in the prizes.

Before leaving the topic of shelter it is worth looking at the lighter wind days when the wind comes off cliffs. If these face the sun there will be thermals lifting up their faces and as the air tends to be stagnant over the face of the cliff and for some distance seaward, the prospect is of a mini-seabreeze streaming towards the cliffs to replace the air carried aloft by the thermals. The wind may not actually blow towards the land where you are, but the component that is trying to blow shorewards being opposed to that which is trying to blow seaward, it can locally reduce inshore waters to fitful puffs and near calms that make for very frustrating sailing. However, these conditions have one advantage in that they clear coastal fog like magic leaving pockets of sunshine right in along the cliffs while everywhere else is clamped out in very poor visibility. If racing an Olympic-style triangle in these conditions make sure you know where you are going on the seaward legs as you will probably not have your passport with you!

25 Coastland Sailing

In this venue you are too far from the actual coastline itself to have the effects that are associated with seabreeze starting up or to experience the thermal bending that was described under the *Inshore* section. However, you are still well within the throw of the seabreeze when it becomes established.

Sailing on long arms of the sea, rivers or lakes cum reservoirs which are some ten miles or more in from the main sea coast means that mostly your winds will be those of inland sites. You will get the gusts and the wind shifts that go with the shelter you have from certain directions or the cant of the local topography. You must read those up under the *Inland* heading. Here we will be describing only those things which are peculiar to the *Coastland* zone.

As seabreezes tend to travel inland behind seabreeze fronts at about 3 knots in the first few hours of their journey from the main coastline so the *Coastland* zone cannot expect to have seabreeze wind shifts until the afternoon. This means they will often coincide with afternoon races except on some otherwise flat-calm days when the seabreeze starts over the beaches as early as 9 a.m. The most likely thing is that a sailing area which is 10 miles (15 kilometres) inland will be experiencing the calming of a wind, that stems from an inland point, around 2–3 p.m., but as it is found that the seabreeze front travels faster during the afternoon (making as much as 8 knots in the middle of the afternoon) those who sail on stretches of water perhaps 30 miles from the coast may expect the breeze somewhere towards tea-time.

To be a little more specific, if the conditions around 9 a.m. are flat calm and the other necessary seabreeze things exist then expect a breeze as early as you ever get it. If the morning wind is from the land and a few knots expect the seabreeze sometime during the afternoon. If the morning wind, however, is approaching 10 knots and is from some inland point you may not experience it at all. Also twenty to thirty miles inland is as far as many seabreezes get before they run out of steam and then the effect is to spread a pregnant calm over the whole area making afternoon sailing a matter of catching odd zephyrs and bits of wind that may sometimes come from inland and at other times from seaward. You are in the front line under these circumstances and while the sun continues to pour energy onto the land there will be stalemate between the land wind and the seabreeze. Eventually however, the land wind has to win because the seabreeze will falter and give way letting the land wind back onto what it considers is its own territory. Once that happens it will be a question of having that wind, but remembering that it also will be going down with evening and you cannot expect to enjoy it for long.

Figure 25.1 *Normal penetration of seabreeze fronts against off-shore wind directions on the East and South Coasts of England. On a few late spring days the fronts may go further than indicated*

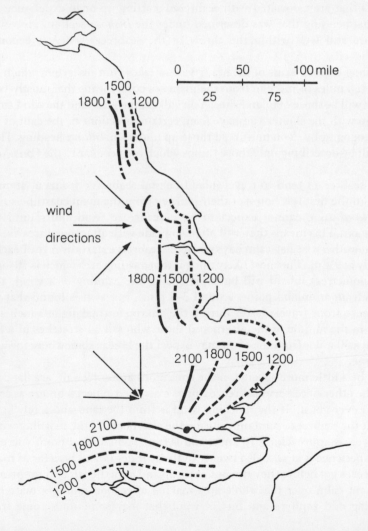

With winds from the direction of the sea you must expect the morning wind to strengthen considerably by afternoon. It may also become showery with all the variability in the wind that that entails. In any case air from the sea tends to be humid and so will often form cloud over the land even if there is none over the sea.

How the seabreeze front moves inland on the South and East coasts of England is shown in Fig. 25.1 and the lines show roughly where the seabreeze wind shift will have got to by the time indicated. Seabreeze fronts move best against winds that are at 45° to themselves so both the South and East coasts will experience maximum seabreeze penetration against the northwesterly that is not too strong. That means a high or a ridge over the Atlantic, feeding cool air down across England. This air will be a brand of mP air and so absolutely perfect for the strong formation of seabreeze fronts.

Winds from other directions such as SW, S or SE do not often have the attributes of instability which means, in simple terms, that heap clouds do not readily grow in them. Thus a north-facing coast, where the seabreeze has to penetrate against winds from these southerly directions, is much less likely to have strong seabreezes and they will not go as far inland as on the coasts that face south or east. West-facing coasts will form seabreeze fronts against easterlies and these are difficult to pin down to any particular degree of stability.

In general, on the spot, if you suspect a good day for seabreezes then look around for cumulus clouds. If there are some and whatever the wind direction, they will indicate that the seabreeze system will be working at its strongest for the conditions that prevail. There can be no precision in timing, but if you know that a seabreeze front and its attendant windshift are likely then you can keep an eye open for signs of it, or even if it catches you unawares you will know what has caused the change in the wind direction.

Once the variable speed and direction phase has passed you can expect a more-or-less steady breeze for at least an hour or two and one that will have very few tactical shifts in it. After that in the *Coastland* zone you have to think of the previous wind coming back and pushing the seabreeze off your sailing patch.

26 Inland Sailing

When recently I went to give a weather talk to board sailors at Grafham Water I was intrigued to talk to a family who learned to sail boards on what sounded to me like a pocket-handkerchief of water that lay not far from their back door. But this is the trend. Wherever there is a piece of water that is just large enough to get some kind of course into and is not forbidden, then there will be the boards if not the dinghies.

The weather for the inland sailor, be it on lake, reservoir or river, is truly land weather and the surface wind will often be entirely different from the gradient wind seen on the weather chart. Sail more than 30 miles (50 km) from the nearest sea coast and you will hardly ever see anything that could be called a seabreeze. However, you may be in a region to where the breeze can just penetrate on good seabreeze days and be visited by late-afternoon calms. You can judge the possibilities of this from Fig. 25.1 which shows the normal distance to which seabreeze fronts penetrate in Britain. Similar venues elsewhere will experience similar seabreeze penetration but, as I pointed out in Chapter 25, the East and South coasts of England are peculiarly attractive for seabreezes and many other coasts do not experience quite the effects that these British ones do.

Otherwise your local winds will be dictated by the local terrain and the shoreside obstructions. Only a contour map and a close look at the shores of the sailing venue will help sort this out for you. Here the idea of following streamlines in winds from different directions over your waters is a good one and can help reveal cants in the wind direction that you might not otherwise have seen to be there.

When sailing inland waters the difference between the speed in gusts and lulls is at its maximum because the lulls are true land wind slowed down by the roughness of the surface. The gusts are gradient wind and when they first arrive from above are not held back by anything. Thus they can drop over the trees into pockets of almost flat calm producing sudden and bad-tempered stabs of wind that have you almost over, or even fully over, only to be lost to almost calm again as the gust hurries on.

If the water lies in a valley, as so many lakes and reservoirs must do, never underestimate the steering effect of that valley and expect there to be more

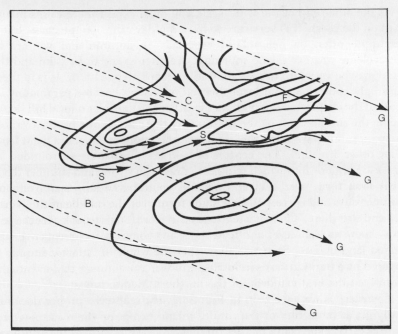

Figure 26.1 *Things that can happen to the surface wind in hilly country when the gradient wind is directed at an angle across a waterway*

winds along the valley than you might think. Also, when the wind is forecast to blow moderate to fresh expect it to funnel into fresh to gale when the flanking hills are at all bluff.

Some of the things that can happen and should be looked for in the lie of surrounding hills and valleys are illustrated in Fig. 26.1. Here we have a lake or reservoir across which the gradient wind (G) is blowing, and surrounding it some not very massive hills. The wind which will be most different from the gradient is the steered wind (S) that blows down the valley in which the waterway lies. Where the contours funnel the wind into a smaller space as at C there is increased speed, but the wind that blows through the confluence must fan out and spread beyond as it is released from its temporary confinement.

Where a substantial hill interposes itself the winds will bifurcate and blow in two entirely different directions. This is illustrated at B while beyond a hill (at L) there may well be a region of lowered wind speed. At F is illustrated falling wind and here we need a steeply rising hillside on the windward side and the wind to be forced to come over it. The wind will not constitute a danger from such a direction until it develops showers or thunderstorms when the impetus given to the descending air by the downdraughts from the showers or storms is very marked. You can find out more about this prospect under 'Highland Sailing'!

At the other end of the wind scale you must expect more calms inland than on the coast. It is very rare to have midday calms on the coast, but it can quite often happen inland especially in autumn and winter. In anticyclonic weather inland mornings are often going to be calm and the wind may be very loth to pick up until perhaps 10 or 11 a.m. It is in these very light conditions that local thermal influences become paramount.

Read the chapters about highland weather and consider if local hill slopes facing the sun may not be the reason why there is a gentle breeze towards them on sunny days when the gradient wind ought to suggest a wind from some other direction. The centres of land masses that are surrounded by water are regions into which winds are drawn on spring and summer days. Heat lows form over central England, central Sweden, Spain etc. on summer days and corresponding highs form over the middle of the North Sea and elsewhere. There is a tendency therefore for air to sink over the sea, flow ashore as seabreezes and feed the rising convection currents over the heated land masses. Statistics show that the whole of Atlantic Europe is covered by a trend towards inflowing winds in the summer that eventually go to feed the heat cauldron of the northern Mediterranean.

However, as we have seen in Fig. 25.1, the seabreeze proper does not really get as far as fifty or sixty miles inland except on the most powerful seabreeze days and could not get there in any case as early as the afternoon so there is another factor at work and this is what I am going to call the 'heat-low drift'. This movement of air to fill a heat low further inland is in the same direction as the seabreeze, but runs ahead of it. It may help the penetration of seabreezes when it occurs, but when you sail an inland waterway of some kind and it is hot and light-variable, the wind that sets in in the afternoon may well be 'heat-low drift' when it is in the right direction.

If not, and an unusual wind springs up, think of thunderstorms in the local area. The heat low will help generate thunderstorms and they may suddenly erupt over inland regions especially where there is some higher ground. In the USA the gigantic storms that breed tornadoes are found to be at their most active when the wind is directed to blow along the axes of the hill ridges and of course it demands that the conditions are hot and humid – true thunder weather. Do not think that the USA is alone in having tornadoes. They may get the really big ones, but lesser tornadoes such as occur in association with bad thunderstorms in England and in Europe, especially Southern Europe, are still too much for small craft.

As shown in Chapter 27, the worst storms come up against the wind that they are drawing towards them to feed their voracious updraughts. If there is thunder heard or lightning seen to leeward then assume that it might be prudent to make for the shore. Storms inland are usually much more active than those near to the coasts or over the sea. There are more of them and they produce the worst conditions. Hail may grow to tennisball size occasionally in such storms well inland, but that is almost unheard of near the coast. There was a tornado at Cowes once but it was some eighty years ago – yet tornadoes happen inland with much greater regularity than you might otherwise think. Unless there is loss of life or substantial damage to property tornadoes are not often reported on the national media although they will be in the local press.

There are regions where big storms are most likely. In Britain the area of greatest frequency is London and the counties surrounding it. Yet as you go north and west the incidence of thunderstorms falls off. They have storms in Wales and Scotland, but they are much less frequent than in central England. Similar situations will obtain in other countries and if you want to know about this it is best to consult a good climatology book for the country or region in question.

Thunderstorms can be divided into three main categories:

i *air-mass storms* – which are single storm cells that grow in cold unstable airstreams or may be caught up in active cold fronts,
ii *frontal storms* – which are broad bands of storms breaking out over a frontal surface such as warm fronts in spring and summer and cold fronts at any time of year,
iii *heat-low storms* – which are the worst storms inland, but are rarely seen on the coasts except when a storm area develops inland and drifts out to sea. However, by that time it has usually lost most of its ferocity.

Apart from the danger of being struck by lightning, which is a pretty improbable occurrence in small boats, there are two major effects of thunderstorms. The most important is the great and sudden increase in wind they may bring. Heat-low storms are the worst for this as the sudden squalls, that can take the wind from less than 10 knots towards the storm to 30–40 knots away from it in a very short time, are generated by the downdraughts where it is raining or hailing most heavily. The falling rain drags down the air with it which spreads around the leading edge of the storm as a whale-back of cold wind whose speed is much greater than any wind actually present in the storm. Here is a case where the wind at the surface is far stronger than that higher up for the storm may be moving at say 20 knots with the winds around two miles up and the downdraught gale may be twice that.

The other important factor is the cold that falling hail and rain bring with them. By definition almost, it is too hot for protective clothing before a big thunderstorm area develops, but the fall in temperature when the precipitation starts is often catastrophic. It may drop 20°F sometimes, that is, go from the eighties into the sixties and that catches all those who have nothing but their skins to protect them. As the storm's squall will also knock most boats or boards over, the risk of danger from exposure increases. Because the water is usually warm at the time of year when these big storms develop, the risk is not as great as it might otherwise be, but you only need one big late spring storm with people unprepared for what is to come and the dangers multiply.

It is an interesting and important fact that the developing thunderstorm moves preferentially along the river valleys or the valleys in which reservoirs have been sited. The reason why is given in Chapter 27, but for now just accept it as a fact and realise that your chances of starting off under the first of the developing storm cells and ending up under the last of them is greater on many inland sailing areas than in surrounding 'dry' areas. Storms will move not with the direction of the surface wind, but with the wind at a mile or two up. So if you want to know which way they are moving watch the flight of altocumulus clouds although stratocumulus nearer the surface may also give away the direction of motion of the storms. This follows because:

i if the winds change greatly in direction with height then the storms cannot get organised and will not be bad ones,

ii with big storms the winds at any level cannot be strong.

If the wind is moderate or above for some time before storms begin to break out then the result will usually be that the storms will not be very bad and will pass relatively quickly. It is the stagnant, humid day when the big storm areas develop and the local winds are often almost entirely generated by the storms themselves. Some idea of what those winds will be is given in the next chapter where we explain the anatomy of them, the better for you to understand what is going on.

27 The Winds of Thunderstorms

Thunderstorms have been mentioned in several of the previous chapters, but not all storms are alike. Some of them break out over the surfaces of warm fronts or occlusions and the towering cumulonimbus clouds sprout upwards through the clouds of the front into the clear air above. Their mushroom-field appearance can only be appreciated by the air traveller (Fig. 27.1). To the sailor there is a great deal of lightning and the thunder crashes and rolls around the sky making in general more noise than the more conventional storms whose bases are near the ground. It is quite normal for these frontal storms to grow from bases that are two or more miles up so that the lightning has difficulty in jumping from cloud to ground and prefers to jump from cloud to cloud. This often results in only the reflection of the flash being seen and we have a display of sheet lightning. Therein lies the well-tried truth that sheet lightning is less dangerous than forked. However, nearly all lightning flashes are forked and when the light reflects off the clouds it apparently spreads out and so is called 'sheet'.

Those flashes that do make it to the ground will be energetic ones, but

Figure 27.1 *The way high-level thunderstorms can break out along warm fronts when the latter move in on the afternoon of a previously hot day*

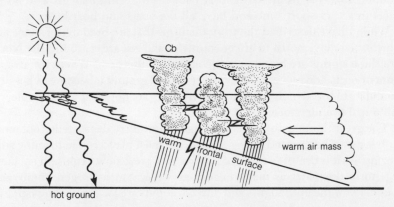

they are far less in number than are to be expected from the more conventional thunderstorm. Thus the frontal storm may not be as bad as the heat storm that breeds inland on hot days. However, here we have to be careful because experience shows that some frontal storms are as bad if not worse than heat storms.

There is a form of frontal storm which invades the English Channel and Southern England from Central France. It is a well-known phenomenon and the weather type before the storms is often one of poor visibility amounting almost to fog. The wind is usually light from the east in the morning and the sky is populated with islands of characteristic altocumulus cloud. These typically form in lines along the wind and out of their tops sprout small turrets or battlements of cloud which give the cloud its scientific name of Ac castellanus. Castellanus is a cloud that forms ahead of thundery conditions and another form is Ac floccus which is easy to remember because the members of the cloud islands look very much like a flock of woolly sheep. These two cloud types (castellanus and floccus) are the ones which warn of coming thundery tendency. It does not have to thunder after they are seen, but certainly these frontal storms from France are nearly always preceded by such clouds.

After a period when it gets very hot the usual pattern is for the upper sky to become covered in cloud from the south and this lowers until the thunder can be heard and then the wind begins to increase. It may blow fresh or even locally strong when the heavy rain comes and the direction may shift in odd ways which it is difficult to describe adequately. The thunder and lightning may appear to be almost continuous and the more there is the worse the conditions become. The whole thing usually passes in a matter of two to three hours.

If you cannot avoid sailing under these frontal storm areas then watch for the darker rolls of cloud that show the leading edges of the storm. That is where there may be big gusts and occasionally instead of the storms growing all over the frontal surface the worst of the conditions forms along what amounts to a cold front. When that happens the wind may grow to 30–40 knots in a very short time and have all the boats and boards over.

While I have described the frontal storms that are bred over France and which then move north to affect countries and sea areas around the North Sea these storms are by no means confined to this area. Whenever a warm front or occlusion moves in above over-heated ground it becomes a possible candidate to breed high-level storms, but they are not what most people will call a real thunderstorm.

The great thunderstorm that breaks out on sultry days needs cool moist air lying over hot ground and so seabreezes must play a roll in forming such storms. As it is useful to think of a storm as a great slow explosion (in fact a big storm dissipates as much energy as a megaton hydrogen bomb) and roughly how the updraughts and downdraughts are located is shown in Fig.

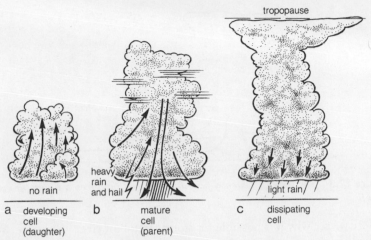

heavy
rain
and hail

no rain

light rain

a developing   b   mature   c   dissipating
   cell   cell   cell
   (daughter)   (parent)

Figure 27.2 *Three stages in the growth of a single thunderstorm cell:*
(a) is a newly-developing cell, probably the daughter of another parent storm
cell (not shown)
(b) a mature cell produces the worst conditions
(c) when an anvil develops the cell is past its prime and the rain is lightening.
However, it will have spawned a daughter to carry on the bad work

27.3. However, if a storm cannot go on getting 'fuel' in the form of moisture
it is bound to die out.

It is useful to understand how a storm starts and then keeps going. When
the upper air is much cooler than the surface over which it lies
upward-going currents need not stop until they hit the tropopause. The
tropopause is the layer at the top of the available atmosphere which prevents
any further ascent of air and so it potentially puts a lid on weather processes.
When the air can no longer ascend it spreads out sideways and forms the
trade-mark of thunderstorms – the anvil. The latter consists of ice-crystals
and so the anvil cloud is called 'false cirrus' (Fig. 27.2c).

The paradoxical thing is that once a stormcloud gets big enough to form
an anvil it is past its prime as a generator of lightning, thunder, hail and rain.
We can resolve this paradox when we realise that a thunderstorm area is a
dynamic mass of individual storm cells with new cells being born from
parents when they are mature.

Briefly, when a storm cell is growing and still has a round and bulging
top, it cascades a mass of heavy rain and hail onto the ground. This falling
water and ice drags down the air with it and the air spreads out around the
cell as a cold whale-back of dense moist air. This lifts the warm air on the
flanks of the mature cell and starts the development of a daughter cell which
grows beside its parent. Then while the parent is going into the senile 'anvil'
stage the daughter cell is growing to maturity keeping the storm going (Fig.
27.3).

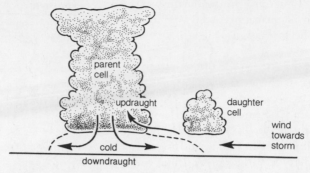

Figure 27.3 *The way in which a parent storm cell produces a daughter cell by its side*

Here we see why it is possible for storms to follow river valleys etc. What happens is that daughter storms will form most readily over the damper terrain and so a storm cell alongside a river, lake or reservoir is more likely to be able to spawn over the moist watery valley than over the drier land. Even if the wind is not very close in direction to the axis of the valley each new generation is likely to be born on the side of the water and so the storm cells develop across the wind and appear to follow the valley (Fig. 27.4).

When big storms develop the conditions have to be pretty stagnant and there has to be very little wind aloft either. Heavy storms cannot possibly grow in winds that are at all strong as the change in wind with height just pulls them apart and does not allow their updraughts and downdraughts to

Figure 27.4 *How a parent cell P spawns a daughter D_1 at position P_1 and on the moist-air side, that is over the waterway or its valley. Daughter D_1 becomes parent P_2 and produces daughter D_2 and so on, so that the storms grow along the valley crab-wise*

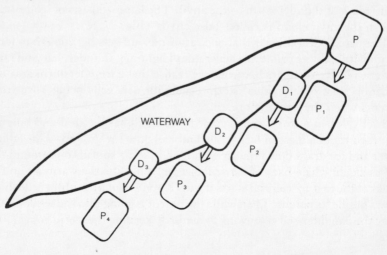

develop. Thus cols are favourite places for storms to breed, while old shallow lows make a prepared bed in which the storms can grow and these prompt the formation of heat lows when they stick over a land mass in summer.

Storms may develop on the foothills of a mountain range or along a hill ridge because the air is given an upward push by having to ascend the hill. This can make air erupt which otherwise would not be unstable. At other times thunderstorms may develop not many miles inland along a particularly active seabreeze front. Air off the sea will be moist and cool – both attributes of air that is ripe to produce showers if not storms – and the beaches may be bathed in sunshine while say 5–10 miles inland it can be raining heavily with lightning stabbing the ground. The storms will pull in air to feed their updraughts and add to the on-shore component of the wind, so quite a strong breeze may develop. It is worth considering whether the on-shore breeze you may have over the *Beachlands* or *Inshore* and which has grown to a strength you are sure is too strong to be a simple seabreeze may not be being enhanced by storms inland.

It might not seem important on the coast to think about the *Inland* sailors suffering under the deluge except that the effect of the big downdraughts is to reverse the wind from into the storms to away from the storms. That downdraught wind can first kill the breeze on the coast and then reverse it making for a cool or even cold evening after what has been a warm day.

While it is impossible to describe all the possible local wind effects that storms can induce it does help to know how the winds usually blow around a travelling storm. We will firstly describe the winds of the big heat storms.

It is a well-known observation that the 'storm comes up against the wind', but when it does that it is going to be a bad storm. This follows because the wind towards the storm is feeding the storm itself. It will usually be less than 10 knots and very hot and sultry. The whole atmosphere feels oppressive – you just know that you are in for trouble. It is evident from Fig. 27.2b that the downdraught comes from high up in the middle of the storm and maybe starts off with a speed of 15–20 knots, but the addition of the downdraught can double that.

There is an arch-cloud over the 'front porch' of the coming storm and under it will certainly be the nose of the cold squall driving out from the storm. The sudden reversal of wind direction and the equally sudden drop in temperature, even if the rain has not started, plus the inky blackness of the cloud arched over the grey waters can all contribute to a possible danger situation, and it is a moment to stay with the boat or board whatever state of soggy uprightness or inversion it has taken.

Contrary to the situation ahead of lesser showers the wind at the head of the storm is backed to the direction of its travel and the strongest squall will be here. The bluster will keep up so there is nothing to do but hang on and hope. As the rain eases so will the wind and as the storm clears and the rain tails away the wind will lighten and back. I have seen the wind behind a storm blowing into it at almost 90° from the left of its line of advance (Fig. 27.5).

Thunderstorms take over the local wind-field almost completely once they get going and when thunder can be heard approaching, even if no lightning is seen at first, expect the wind to shift at the behest of the coming monster. If it drifts towards, consider whether it would not be best to get ashore, and if it continues to come from the storm then expect more wind once the storm gets close (Fig. 27.6).

The cell theory of thunderstorms tells us to look for the individual cells if we are to make any predictions of the wind to come. This may be rather difficult as the cold air spreading round the storm not only builds full-scale daughter cells, but also much peripheral cumulus cloud which tends to hide the true nature of what is behind it. So look for the tops which may be visible above the nearer cloud. Great bulbous heads with small knobs on like a cauliflower indicate cells in their prime, while anvils indicate older parent cells. Both will be present when a full-scale storm is in progress, but sometimes lesser storms, far more individual and isolated, will have nothing apparently other than an anvil top, though look around and you may well see new storm clouds building near to those whose anvils make them so very conspicuous.

Figure 27.5 *The anatomy of a big storm*

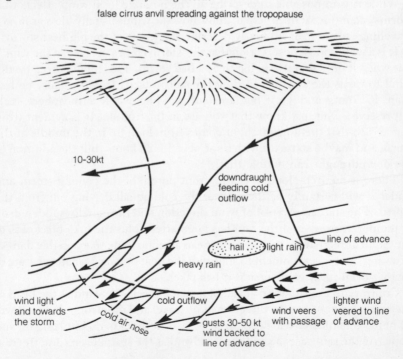

false cirrus anvil spreading against the tropopause

10-30kt

downdraught feeding cold outflow

line of advance

hail   light rain

heavy rain

wind light and towards the storm

cold air nose

cold outflow

gusts 30-50 kt wind backed to line of advance

wind veers with passage

lighter wind veered to line of advance

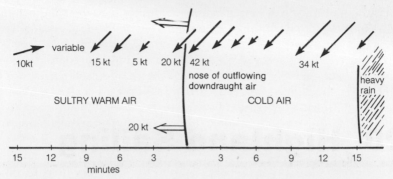

Figure 27.6 *The winds for 15 minutes before and 15 minutes after the cold squall at the head of a big thunderstorm. The wind at first was 10 knots towards the storm, but 10 minutes before the big squall it turned round. Compare the winds here with those of a shower in Fig. 7.2*

The bad heat storm can generate tornadoes and in the United States the sign they look for in the storm clouds is a form of cloud called Mamma. It is so-named because it looks like a mass of teatless cows' udders hanging down around the edges of the main cloud. Once you have seen this cloud you will not forget it, but do not think that every cumulonimbus that has accompanying mammatoform clouds will produce a whirlwind. In Britain and like latitudes mamma often forms behind a departing storm cloud and I have seen it under a cold front that was passing over. Interestingly enough small whirlwinds can wriggle down from unstable high clouds and affect the wind at the surface as I once experienced while sailing in Chichester Harbour. There was a sudden loss of wind and then the boat gybed of its own accord and I found we were sailing in the opposite direction temporarily. I looked up and there above was this little snake of cloud hanging below the grey cloudbase. It was not bad – just strange.

Only those who sail *Inshore* waters stand any prospect of experiencing waterspouts, which are far more prevalent than tornadoes and are often seen in the Mediterranean and quite often in the English Channel when the conditions are very unstable. However, I have never met anyone who was swept by a waterspout while sailing a dinghy inshore so the risk is quite small.

28 Highland Sailing

Before starting on this chapter I must remind the reader of the definition of 'highland' adopted for this book. The term means that the sailing venue is considerably affected by surrounding hills and valleys, but that does not mean that you have to necessarily be on a finger lake in the Alps although we shall mention such places in passing.

Generally the winds over highland lakes and reservoirs will be guided by the local contours far more when the skies are overcast or it is, say, cloudless and cold than when the air is lumpy with cumulus, cumulonimbus or other forms of heap clouds. The air over hilly terrain develops cloud very easily and there is often a total cover of dark grey turbulence cloud which has grown because the ups and downs of the hills has induced ups and downs in the airstream. Such airstreams are full of micro-shifts, but very few of them are predictable and so studying the lie of the land and drawing some streamlines on a rough contour map you have culled from the appropriate large-scale local map will be far more rewarding than trying to play the shifts. In this connection look at the things that may happen in Fig. 26.1.

Big lakes in highland settings will have local winds that often get names because of the regularity with which they turn up over certain parts of the lake. Look for large-scale steering effects due to hill or mountain 'walls' that stretch along the lengths of many such lakes and do not imagine that a truly formidable barrier cannot affect the run of the wind several miles away from it. Also realise that winds canalised by mountain or hill ridges increase in strength very often so that as winds pick up from the 'bad weather' quarter they may do so with greater speed and from a more consistent direction than on lowland waters.

The daytime wind that has blown because the isobars are directed that way may well keep going well into the evening due to the effect of anabatic winds on slopes that lie far away or even out of sight up the valley at the head of the lake or reservoir. Equally, early morning winds that blow at the behest of katabatics down the valleys and feed into the lake can be materially aided by a developing gradient and so become quite strong. Such effects go against the diurnal changes considered normal by people brought up on lowland and coastal sites (see 'Mountain and Valley Winds', page 149).

When the conditions go quiet but the sun shines, there will be lake breezes that are the equivalent of seabreezes, but they will in general be weak compared to the seabreeze. They will grow towards the slopes in the sun and quickly fade when those slopes move into shadow. At night there can be slight nocturnal winds onto shores that look back to a flat hinterland for several miles, but if the land rises within a relatively short distance then night-time katabatic winds reinforce any land breeze tendency and the wind from the shore becomes appreciable. It is in quiet conditions that local knowledge will pay off and if you do not know the waters then follow someone who does.

Turning to the other extreme, look out for the effects of falling winds even when the ground is some miles away. A substantial hill or mountain barrier that thwarts the build-up of westerly or southwesterly winds in the circulation of depressions can add two or more Beaufort forces to the wind you might expect from the isobars and then it is possible that a Force 8 gale will become Force 10 due to the wind falling down the slopes.

If there are any snow-capped peaks within range then allow for mistral-type squalls when cold polar air blows over them and so onto the water. Snowy tops must always make you think of the sudden arrival of heavy squalls which could be quite literally out of the blue. They may not happen, but you should find out what the chances are.

Mountain and Valley Winds

It almost goes without saying that lakes and reservoirs set in hilly or mountainous regions will generally be elongated in one or more directions and the ends of the waterway will look up a valley and down a valley respectively. Thus lakes are very susceptible to the winds that are produced by the anabatic and katabatic winds which are in turn produced from slopes in sun and shadow. The wind to replace the rising anabatic drift up a sunlit hillside will be a surface one tending to hug the contours and so will often be drawn from the lake or reservoir. The general rules as to when the winds will blow up and down valleys as the day progresses are summed up in Fig. 28.1 which is based on one originally drawn by F. Defant in 1949.

At sunrise the mountain wind is blowing down from the mountains onto the water (a), but as the sun climbs in the early forenoon the opposing tendency to blow back towards the mountains cancels the early morning wind and calm prevails (b). By the early afternoon the wind is now blowing up the valley in response to the anabatics induced by the sun's rays (c). This continues into the late afternoon and evening, but the calm returns in the early night as the sinking (katabatic) tendency now cancels the momentum of the valley wind that was blowing earlier (b). The mountain wind settles in to blow in the middle of the night and continues through the early hours and on through sunrise until once again its momentum is killed by the trend towards wind back towards the mountains.

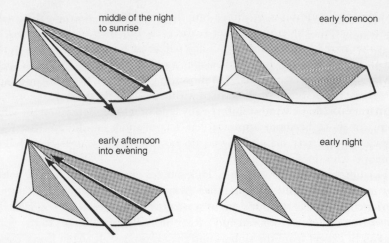

Figure 28.1 *The daily shift of the mountain and valley wind system*

These mountain and valley winds are almost large-scale and may blow even when the water is covered in cloud or fog because the slopes that command the valleys are in sunshine. However, when the slopes local to the waterside are in sun then an anabatic drift towards them must be added to any valley wind trend (Fig. 28.2.a). It could be that on calm mornings the only wind there is will be due to local lake breezes because any larger-scale valley wind has not yet materialised. In the afternoon when the sun has greatest power there may be a fight between local lake breezes and valley winds, but by late afternoon or evening the katabatic tendency from slopes previously in sun can produce off-shore lake breezes which again must be considered in relation to any valley wind that is still blowing (b).

Downdraught Winds

These are usually the result of thunderstorms, but heavy showers without any thunder can also produce the effects. Most wind is horizontal, but when a deluge of rain cascades out of the base of a cumulonimbus cloud it drags the air down with it. Thus strong descending air currents come down with the rain. Over horizontal ground they splay out round the base of the cloud and account in part for the often upsetting squalls that accompany showers. However, get them over a steep hillside and then their force is not spent in useless collision with the ground, but comes racing down the hillside as a downdraught gale (Fig. 28.3).

Often before such downdraught gales occur it is more than usually calm, which makes the contrast between the conditions before and after even more striking. The wind from them may spread across a coastal plain from mountains inland sweeping away any other breezes that are blowing, but when this happens the friction of the land controls the wind speed. Not so on high lakes and reservoirs where the steep sides rise almost sheer out of the water. Then the downdraught gale is on you before you know it or possibly even suspect it. Off sea coasts under cliffs similar falling winds can produce downdraught gales, but undoubtedly the greater danger is to be found on lakes, tarns, fjords etc. which are set in clefts in the mountains.

Föhn Winds

These are specifically warm, dry southerlies blowing down the Alpine valleys, but while they find their greatest ferocity in that locality winds with

Figure 28.2 *(a) In the morning, slopes in the sun will promote anabatic winds and on-shore drift will occur even with the lake still in shadow*
(b) Late afternoon or early evening sees slopes once in sunlight now lost in shadow and katabatic winds develop so producing off-shore drift

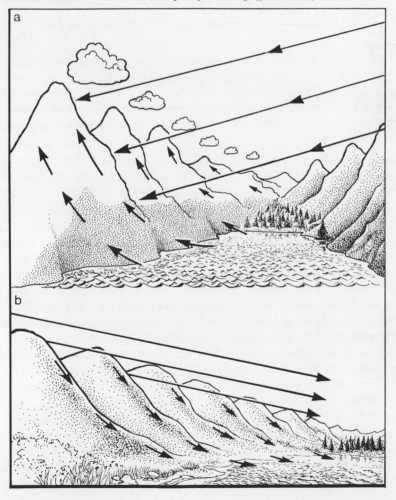

Figure 28.3 *How downdraught gales occur over the steep sides of mountain lakes etc*

föhn characteristics can be found anywhere where air is forced to scale a substantial ridge and so sink and warm up as it descends the other side. The föhn is a very dry warm wind and the reason for this is that when depressions move north of the Alps they bring in moist southerlies. The moist air lifted up on the Mediterranean slopes produces much cloud and rain there and cools at half the rate that it will warm up by when it has lost its moisture content and comes winging down the Alpine valleys. Thus it arrives on the north side hot and dry and with a ferocity that has got it a very bad name. (Fig. 28.4a).

Unnaturally fine weather precedes the onset of föhn so that the mountains appear very close. The sky around the further mountain peaks may appear to have a green tinge and be peopled by small elongated clouds. The pre-föhn conditions can last for days before the first hot blasts herald the onset of a föhn gale. Lakes that lie in a direction that looks into the mountains will be most prone to föhn gales.

The similar wind of the American Rockies is the Chinook which can raise the high plains at the eastern foot of the Rockies from freezing to 40°F in fewer minutes. Again, in Britain föhn effects keep Aberdeen on the east Scottish coast very warm at times when moist air is forced across the Grampian Highlands by a depression to the north. Similarly the coastal plain between Liverpool and Lancaster sometimes gains record temperatures when the wind blows from NE or E over the backbone of the Pennines. There are going to be many places in the lee of mountain ridges which will also experience föhn effects, but one of the most important aspects of them has not been covered and it is a psychological one. In hospitals in the areas prone to föhn they suspend important (and non-critical) operations because the pre-föhn as well as the actual föhn conditions are known to induce erratic behaviour leading for example, to a proved correlation between föhn and traffic accidents as well as producing alarming increases in suicides both actual and attempted. The cause may be

Figure 28.4 *(a) The situation that leads to föhn in Alpine valleys. (b) The situation that leads to mistral-type winds. The Bora is much the same situation*

traceable to a surfeit of positive electric ions in the air and many situations where there are sudden breaks in weather conditions close to the ground produce similar bad effects on the human psyche. These can include any hot dry winds for any cause and the scirocco of the Mediterranean is well known as producing ill effects when it arrives in southern Italy and Sicily etc. with temperatures well over 100°F. Other ionic disturbers of the peace are of course thunderstorms which are normally negatively charged in their bases and so induce opposite positive charge in the surface and objects on the surface. The passage of sharp cold fronts may induce temporary lapses on the part of helmsmen which added to the sudden squally shift of wind, could result in a capsize that otherwise would not have occurred. When it has been cool for days and suddenly it goes hot, take extra care in driving to the club, rigging the craft, sailing the race – you might be the victim of a föhn-type breakdown in your normally impeccable reactions. It need not result in any greater disaster than losing a race you wanted to win, but recognition that a weather-based psychological effect is possibly in being could have you concentrating harder and thereby mitigating its more adverse effects.

Mistral and Bora Type Winds

Just as it is possible to find lesser föhn-type winds wherever mountain ridges stand athwart warm moist winds, so you do not have to necessarily sail the Mediterranean coast between Perpignan on the Spanish Border and the Gulf of Genoa to experience forms of mistral. However, the mistral is the archetype of the mountain wind that comes when the pressure pattern is orientated to bring winds from the north side of the Alps. Its name implies that it is a masterful wind that sweeps away other more favourable winds there may be and certainly this is so because there are, on average, some six to fourteen days in any month when mistral may blow at Force 6 and even during the summer months there is an average two days a month when Force 8 can be expected (Fig. 28.4b).

The mistral is a mountain gap wind which needs the gradient wind to be from some point north. Cool air builds on the north slopes of the Massif Central and the Alps and eventually bursts through the gaps, that is, mainly the Rhône valley and the Garonne gap. Being cold it falls down through the Rhône valley and often under clear skies rises to gale force with very intense gusts. In fact when sailing the Cote d'Azur you must always allow for strong gusty winds from the mountains. The likelihood of mistral will be referred to on the local radio programmes and whenever pressure is low over northern Italy and high over Biscay there is the risk of mistral on what is often, from the travel brochures, assumed to be a coast of perfect weather.

There are pointers here to look for in other venues. For the mountain gap wind to become strong we need:

i a mountain gap somewhere to the north which can look down through connecting valleys to the sailing venue,

ii a weather chart with fairly tight isobars for wind from a northern direction,

iii the wind to be cool already.

A certain amount of katabatic influence helps the mountain gap wind which may not reach gale force, but can come sweeping down through lesser terrain to have unsuspecting sailors capsized into cold, but previously relatively calm, lake or reservoir waters.

To sum up: the mistral-type winds need cool northerlies while the föhn needs warm southerlies.

The Bora is a similar mountain gap wind on the Trieste shore of the Adriatic.

29 Seeing the Wind

As the wind is invisible it may seem amazing to the uninitiated that we can sail in it at all and with such apparent precision. However, the boat or the board is itself a good arrow for the wind and it is on this that we mainly rely.

Dinghies tend to be able to sail at 45° to the true wind direction when they are 'on the wind', that is close hauled on either tack. So we turn the boat towards the wind direction until the luff of the foresail or mainsail begins to show signs of shivering and backwinding and then by bearing away a little we know we are about as close to the wind as we can get.

This way we make way to windward in a series of 'dog's legs', each of which makes roughly a right angle with the previous one. When on the wind, however, we cannot set the boat or board on a course towards a point on the shore and just sail along it regardless. We know that the wind is always moving a little backwards and forwards about the direction we know as the 'mean wind' and if the course is not constantly corrected then sometimes the sails will be shivering by being too close to the wind and at other times heeling is induced because the wind is coming from a freer direction.

It is the helmsman's goal to keep the sails drawing at their best angle to the wind as its shifts backwards and forwards about the mean wind direction. Yet you cannot see the next shift that is about to blow across the craft and can only react when it actually crosses the bow of a dinghy with a foresail or when it meets the luff of the sail on a board. It is amazing how expertly boards are sailed and in winds where dinghies may be giving up when even the help of a shivering foresail luff is not there to be a trigger for a reaction. Obviously familiarity, agility and a measure of intuition will separate the top board and dinghy sailors from the others, but it can also help to have a picture in your mind of how the wind is constructed. That is easier said than done however, because the ways we have of drawing 'pictures' of the wind variations are only analogues of the real thing and need to be converted in our mind from apparently meaningless squiggles on paper to meaningful shifts and speed changes.

A device that senses wind speed is an anemometer and there are several different kinds to be had. The ones which might be of use to dinghy and board sailors are either hand-held cup anemometers or the Ventimeter. The former have three or four cups rather like half table-tennis balls which spin round on top and a dial of some kind which registers the wind speed. The Ventimeter is a slightly tapering vertical plastic tube into the bottom of which the wind blows. A plastic disc slides up and down on a central wire and where it rises to is a measure of the wind speed. As it is completely enclosed and floats if dropped in the water it has certain advantages over the more complicated cup anemometer.

Neither of these devices will however give you a permanent record of what the wind has done. For that we have to have a full-blown recording anemograph. There are two major kinds supplied to met. offices and other places where a constant record is required. One is the electric recorder and the other the pressure tube device. The kind of anemograph that drew the originals of the wind records (anemograms) that are used in this book is one of the latter, but the traces from either look the same. Briefly the pressure tube anemograph has an open-ended tube looking into the wind. The tube transfers the wind's pressure variations to a float chamber rather like a diving bell. The bell rises when the air pressure in it increases and on its top it has a pen so that (as is natural) higher wind speed is shown by a higher trace on the chart. The wind direction is drawn by a pen connected through cams to the shaft at whose head is the wind-vane and it is arranged that winds that veer (that is, move clockwise in direction) appear higher on the trace of wind direction. As the vane swings backwards and forwards so the pen moves up and down in sympathy and a chart on a clockwork-driven drum moves under the pens. In this way permanent records of wind speed and direction are obtained at many places throughout the world. It is from these records that the statistics of wind for any place are calculated.

Once you learn to read them they also tell a great deal about the way the way the wind behaves. A very typical example of twenty-four hours of brisk sailing wind recorded by a pressure tube anemograph at Thorney Island in Chichester Harbour on the south coast of England in July 1952 is Fig. 29.1. Because of the ways of met. offices the day begins around 9 a.m. and so

Figure 29.1 *A typical trace from an anemograph showing 24 hours of brisk sailing wind during high summer on the South Coast of England*

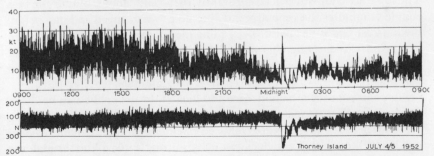

therefore do most anemograms. At this time the wind was blowing at about 16 knots (top of Force 4), but with many gusts and lulls in it so that sometimes it was over 30 knots and at others dropping right down to about 5 knots. The direction was constantly shifting over a span of 100° from a mean direction of NE. This day, because of its strength there was no real sign of a seabreeze force acting against the wind and diminishing it. The only sign of such action is that the wind did not increase as much in the middle of the afternoon as one would have expected and then, as usually happens after late afternoon, it began to drop progressively in speed and veered a little in direction to come from nearer to E. The wind sank to around 5 knots at midnight but it was still variable. Then suddenly there was a big gust which took the wind from about 3 knots or so to over 25 knots. At the same time the wind backed with a bang going right round through N to end up SSW for a time before climbing back to what it was before. This very nasty night-time rogue gust was found to be due to waves sent out from thunderstorms over the western end of the Channel and transported through the night inversion rather as if the latter were a stretched rubber sheet which had been struck hard at one side so that ripples ran across it. At about forty minutes past midnight the 'sheet' ruptured and allowed the wind above the inversion to come down onto the surface.

Then, after some long-period undulations, the wind went back to being what it had been before, showing that whatever caused the curious behaviour of the wind after midnight was imposed by some outside cause – as it proved on investigation to be.

In these and other ways we can study what the wind did and so we can hope to propound some theories as to what it might do in the future.

Most of the time the charts are moved under the pens at a slow rate because details of the wind over intervals of a few seconds are not required. However, by using faster chart-drum speeds the way the wind varies from moment to moment can be seen. Those are the anemograms which are of use to sailing people because every few seconds a canny helmsman is correcting his course to take advantage of the microwind shifts.

So let us look at just four minutes of wind (Fig. 29.2) which will provide the important details that anemograms like Fig. 29.1 cannot possibly show. The top trace shows the speed constantly rising and falling, but for the first couple of minutes the general trend is to go down in speed and just before the big gust it is at its lowest speed. The idea of gust cells, to be described later, will explain why this should be. After that, despite a couple of temporary quiet periods, the wind is above the mean speed. So the second half is part of a gust that lasted for over two minutes.

Now compare the direction trace and look at the mean line that has been drawn through it. It makes a wave form with the crests of the wave being times when the wind was veered (shifted clockwise) and the troughs when it was backed (or shifted anticlockwise). By putting a mean line through the

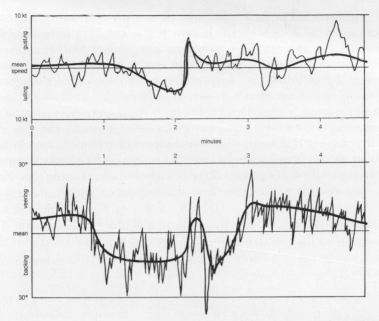

Figure 29.2 *Four minutes of wind speed and direction on an unstable day*

speed trace at the top you will see that the latter also follows the same rough wave form, but not quite so smoothly, the oddity being the sudden gust just after two minutes had elapsed. However, note for future references how the wind veered sharply as this gust occurred. It backed just after and then had to swing more-or-less slowly back through the mean wind direction to end up, after three minutes, veered.

Thinking about sailing a dinghy or board through this wind (and this is a real example and not made up) we see small variations occupying a few seconds plus larger variations covering periods of twenty seconds or so as well as the wave-like changes that occupy several minutes. To understand what this anemogram means in practice, look at the direction trace and imagine you are helming your craft through this wind. Grab an imaginary tiller and forge an imaginary course thinking of the time involved between one shift and the next. You will probably try to meet every shift but find it impossible, as happens in practice. Here you have the unique benefit of knowing which shift is coming next – something you never know when out there finding a way through the variations. If you end up realising that there are aspects of the real wind that you must ignore then it will have been a useful exercise.

We see that many minor changes in the wind are so short-lived that no meaningful response can be made to them. They meet the luff, hurry across the sails and are gone before you can do anything about them. Sometimes they come from the beam and make for an unexpectedly sudden heel, but next moment the wind is back to normal or they can come from ahead but are gone before you can think of bearing away.

The variations that last for a second or two are due to small eddies produced by collision with surface objects and are called turbulence. Turbulent eddies are a great nuisance to sailors who are trying to make sense of the wind because they tend to mask the bigger, more permanent, eddies which have shifts that can be described as 'tactical'.

A tactical wind shift is one where the change in direction is of long enough duration for real advantage to be taken of the shift, or for a tack to be made so that an adverse shift on one tack can be turned to advantage on the other.

Research has shown that apart from the miniscule turbulent eddies there are:

i short eddies – less than 1–2 minutes in duration,
ii medium eddies – with durations of 2–8 minutes,
iii long eddies – that are 5–15 miles in the direction of their motion and so may take half and hour or more to pass.

There is a rule of thumb which says that it takes a second a foot to tack. Therefore the time from when a helsman decides to put his helm down, the boat comes about and then settles and is drawing on the new tack, will vary in dinghies from some ten to twenty seconds. There will be those who say they can go quicker than this and that may well be so, but it is still a useful rule because it helps us sort out the tactical from the non-tactical shifts. When racing we will also have to add some 'decision' time. The helmsman has to warn his crew that he is coming about and then actually do it so maybe we need to add some seconds to the above. Even so the time will be less than half a minute and the shortest eddies we have listed above occupy that kind of time or rather more.

Let's take an example. A 14-foot dinghy is hard on the wind on port tack when a sudden stab of wind comes from ahead forcing her to bear away and so lose windward advantage. The rules of the game say:

Tack on headers.

So wasting no time she tacks. The whole operation takes about twenty to thirty seconds and hardly has she settled on the new starboard tack, but the wind shifts ahead again forcing another tack. Such short tacking can, if premeditated, be something one engages in during ding-dong battles up lee shores, but when it is suddenly forced on one by the wind shifting ahead twice (or sometimes more than twice) in a matter of a minute, it will often result in loss of way and a real feeling of confusion on the part of the members of the crew. Such panic tacking at the behest of a rule is best avoided and so 'Tack on headers' is not a rule you can follow slavishly to the letter as you will soon learn once you have tacked yourself to a standstill in an airstream bristling with short eddies.

To avoid falling too often into the 'Tack on headers' trap you must try to build up a picture in your mind of what the real tactical medium eddies look like as they hurry invisibly through the fleet plus the weather conditions that go with them. But before leaving short eddies these will sometimes form part of the wind-shift system of medium eddies and so they can be useful heralds of a coming tactical wind shift that you can use to your advantage once you know what shifts to expect. Otherwise short eddies must be met, savoured and, when found wanting, ignored except as an undulation in the course being steered.

Gusts and Lulls

Back in the late 1920s, when the Royal Aircraft Establishment were having a honeymoon with the ill-fated airship, they did some research into the way the wind varied under different weather conditions. The idea was to provide some understanding of how gusts and lulls came about and thereby aid the construction of airship masts. What they discovered, however, went far beyond what the boffins at Cardington (Bedfordshire) needed, but it has been of very great value to us as dinghy and board sailors because for the first time they found out what made the medium eddies. They discovered that these eddies were convective in nature and looked like great invisible non-rigid airships themselves. They called each of these monster eddies a 'gust cell' because in its head there is a sudden sharp increase in wind speed (a gust) which keeps up for a minute or two and then more-or-less slowly subsides into a more variable, but lower speed phase (the lull).

If you can recall a gusty day you may remember that the periods of heavy wind that had you using all your resources to hold the boat or board up came in a more-or-less ordered sequence. It is very rare to have to meet two gusts one after another. Each gust phase is usually followed by a lull phase. When you come to think of it this must be so because if most of the phases were gusts then the mean wind speed would be the same as the gusts – in which case you would not be able to recognise the gusts as increases in the mean wind speed. So it is imperative that stronger wind phases are followed by lighter wind phases.

More importantly, for tactical sailing, the same can be said about the wind direction. If there is a mean wind direction this implies immediately that there must be times when the wind is shifted clockwise (veered) to the mean and an equal number of times when it is shifted anticlockwise (backed). These veering and backing shifts might come along as turbulence or short eddies and often they do, but if the veered part of the wind pattern was of several minutes' duration – about the same as the backed part – then tacking to the wind pattern would not only be useful, but imperative, if maximum windward way were to be made.

The Cardington research showed that the gust cell brings down fast-moving air from above and drops it like a parcel into the surface wind-field with its speed and direction intact. This sudden arrival of air from above means that the wind grows suddenly from say 10 knots to 20 knots and stays that way for several minutes. Being undisturbed, air from above has very little turbulence in it. Here is one reason we are able to meet the gusts so well – because although the wind may be at its strongest it is much steadier than it will become as it lightens.

The gust parcel moves on and the wind reverts to what it really wants to be, that is, surface air full of turbulent eddies and slowed by the surface obstacles that created the turbulence. This is the lull and Fig. 29.3 shows an idealised portrait of a couple of gust-lull sequences each one being the wind at the surface due to a single gust cell. Idealised or not, this diagram gives the facts we know about gust-lull sequences:

i the wind just before the gust is at its slowest,
ii the wind speed rises suddenly at the 'gust front',
iii it stays up in speed for something like a couple of minutes,
iv it has very little turbulence in it,
v after the gust phase the wind goes down more-or-less gradually into the lull phase and becomes much more full of microwind shifts.

This information would not be all that important to small-boat sailors, who are trying to find the shortest time around the buoys, were it not for the accompanying wind-shift pattern that goes with the speed pattern. Without going into why at this stage, we can say:

Figure 29.3 *An idealised portrait of two gust-lull sequences in an unstable airstream. Each gust-lull is due to the passage of one gust cell. While no airstream will be as regular as this the diagram gives the facts that are worth knowing. Read the direction trace (b) in conjunction with the speed trace (a)*

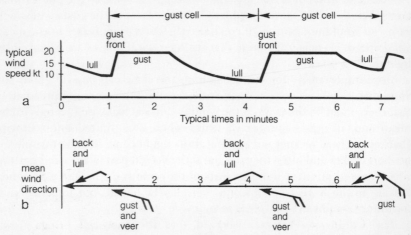

a during the gust phase the wind is shifted clockwise (veered) to the mean direction (NH),

b in the lull phase it shifts back anticlockwise ending up backed to the mean wind direction (NH).

(For the SH for veer read back and vice versa.)

In Fig. 29.3b are shown the facts about the direction shifts that accompany the gusts and lulls. The wind veers as the gust strikes and stays veered for a time after which it may go back suddenly as the wind lulls or, more commonly, it goes back in a series of shifts as the wind falls in speed.

It is the wind shift that goes with each phase of a gust-lull pattern that makes the recognition of what constitutes a tactical airstream so important. You cannot help being made aware of a sizeable gust when it strikes and as it does so you can expect the wind to shift clockwise and so favour starboard tack when beating to windward (NH). It will shift anticlockwise (back) in the SH and so favour port tack. Having said which, so as not to confuse the text with inserts for readers in the Southern Hemisphere, the variations will be given a special section to themselves (page 185).

Equally as the wind lulls, port tack becomes more and more favoured. So if you come to recognise the tactical airstream with gust cells in it then you can hope to go one better than 'Tack on headers' by attempting (other factors like sea room being allowed for) to tack in phase with the gusts and lulls as they are met. We shall see how to recognise such airstreams when we describe the way gust-cells are made and how they operate.

Gust Cells

One way of understanding how the gust cell brings along the gust-lull sequences in a variable airstream is to imagine one of those First World War tanks with their great trapezoidal tracks. We imagine the upper air, which is clear of surface friction, being anchored to the descending track at the head of the gust cell 'tank' and to be continuously splashing onto the surface at G (Fig. 29.4). This air is travelling faster than the air that was just ahead of it and is the gust. Because it arrives from above it barges into the surface wind and there is a sudden increase in wind speed. Until this air has lost its momentum by colliding with surface objects it will continue to blow at a higher than average speed. As the gust cell travels over you the air, that originally came down from above and was cool, warms up by contact with the ground. At the after end of the gust cell it is warm enough to lift off, carried up, in our tank analogy, by the track at the rear to recirculate perhaps 2000–3000 feet up and come down later in another gust. The slowest wind (L) is where it is lifting away at the rear of the cell.

The proportions of a tank will, when expanded to about a mile long, give a good idea of how big one gust cell may be and following it and surrounding it there will be others. Every bit of a field of wind must have wind of some

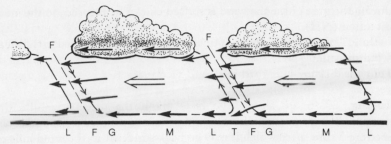

Figure 29.4   *The 'tank-track' analogy to the mechanism of a gust cell*

kind because we know from experience that we do not normally find calm 'holes' in winds that are blowing Force 3–5. So we visualise the cells in plan view rather like Fig. 29.5 and in between one cell and the next is a miniature cold front (F in Fig. 29.4). These gust fronts make it possible for ascending warm air to be on one side and descending cool air on the other.

Because convection is going on in the rear of each cell so there is every chance that a cumulus cloud will result over the cell and show where it is. Every individual Cu cloud is a sign of a gust cell beneath it and so also of a shift pattern that can be expected to perform in certain ways. I know from personal experience that you can easily make up places by keeping an eye on the leading edges of cumulus clouds sailing over, and thereby responding to the gusts before other people. In competitive racing seconds count and he who divines the shifts first has the best chance of using them to advantage. Gust recognition is particularly important when off the wind where short dinghies may not be planing in the lulls, but will be when the gusts strike and he who planes first, often planes past other people. Or when the wind is a bit too strong for comfort and you are planing away in what you recognise as a lull it is very useful to be able to have crew and helmsman ready for the first critical moments of the screaming plane you are about to experience.

Figure 29.5   *Plan of a typical field of gust cells travelling to the left. The +
signs are where air is mainly rising and the − signs are where it is sinking. The
thick lines are the gust fronts G while T is a gust tongue*

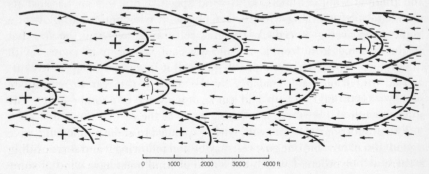

Another way to recognise the onset of gusts is by the reaction of other craft upwind and it is worth noting that in a wind speed of 20 knots it takes 10 seconds for a gust to travel 100 yards. Assuming dinghies have 20-foot masts, one is 100 yards from you when its mast fits from the knuckle to the tip of your thumb held at arm's length. Seeing another boat at this distance careening to a gust gives you enough warning – even to crash-tack if necessary.

Immediate warning of a gust may be 'splash' marks on the water and sometimes when the airstream is too dry to produce tell-tale cumulus clouds these are your only reliable guide to the imminent arrival of a gust. At the other end of the cloud spectrum the cumulus clouds can spread out into stratocumulus that tends to cover the sky and then individual details of the clouds become lost so that you cannot tell what is a leading edge of a cloud where the gust should be. However, the airstream under Sc cloud cover is bound to be less predictably variable and without doubt the airstream that is most likely to reward you for its study is the one dotted with individual Cu clouds. The most likely direction will be NW and it will feel cool for the time of year. This last is bound to be so because for convection currents to occur the air has to be cooler than the ground or sea.

We can make a rule:

Individual lumps of cloud mean individual lumps of wind.

Why the Wind Veers as it Gusts

At first sight you may not be prepared to believe that there is a definite trend in the wind shifts as gusts strike and an opposite one as the wind subsides in speed, but it certainly is true.

It comes about because of the difference between the direction of surface wind and gradient wind (page 57). As pointed out very early in this book the surface wind is often very different in direction from the wind that blows in the direction of the isobars.

In Fig. 29.6a at (A) the surface wind S and the gradient wind G are shown in relation to one another. The surface wind is directed at an angle in towards low pressure while the gradient wind is not. Thus when as at (B) the gradient wind (g) is brought down by descending currents it must be shifted clockwise to the surface wind. The latter is slowed by friction and so is recognised as the air in the lulls (l). These must appear backed in direction to the lumps of gradient wind from above.

Now when the wind suddenly increases it can only be doing so because faster wind from above is involved. That wind must itself be shifted clockwise (veered) to the wind before it, and when it hits you pure there is a gust and a veer. However, sometimes it is pushing slower wind ahead of it and therefore not every increase in speed will have an accompanying veer. Yet on the whole they do and if the leading edges of cumulus clouds can be used to denote where the true gusts are then the shift that gives a lift on

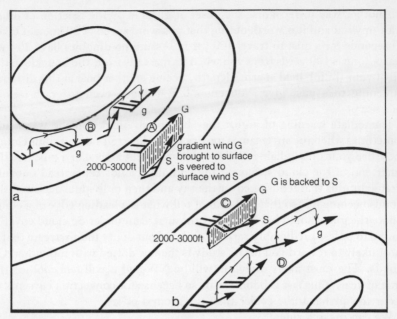

Figure 29.6 *Why the gusts are veered and the lulls backed to the mean wind direction (between the two and not shown) in (a) the NH and (b) the SH*

starboard tack can be expected as well. Equally, after the gust has passed the wind that is left is surface wind that must be backing and so favouring port tack.

In the Southern Hemisphere situation (Fig. 29.6b) we see at (C) that the gusts must be backed to the surface wind and so port tack will be favoured in the gusts and starboard tack in the lulls – exactly the opposite of the Northern Hemisphere situation. Therefore, although I have never sailed in the Southern Hemisphere, the gust reactions to the wind shifts in unstable airstreams must be different in the two hemispheres and those brought up to instinctively react to the shifts in the NH must find a disadvantage in the SH and vice versa.

30 Beating in the Northwesterly

One of the most incisive chapters in any book I have read concerning variable winds and the tactical reactions to them is that by an American, Stuart H. Walker in the book he edited called *The Techniques of Small Boat Racing*. To me this is still, after twenty years (the British edition came out in 1962), a bible which is hard to better. His chapter 'Beating in Varying Northwesters' describes the 'northwesterly' thus:

'"Northwesterly" is used herein as a generic term referring to land breezes characterised by vertical instability and a pronounced variation in direction. They may appear in any given area as winds from directions other than the northwest, but on the Atlantic Coast of North America are characteristically from this direction.'

These words will do for any area where the northwest wind has to blow over the land and so is good for most of Europe, other than the west coasts that face the wind. If you have a land fetch and the northwesterly blows it will have the same characteristics as in North America, no matter where you are around the temperate latitudes of the Northern Hemisphere. Go to the Southern Hemisphere and the same wind will be the southwesterly and in either case these variable winds with predictable shifts in them will be found most often in the rear of departing depressions. The shape of depressions as outlined in Chapter 13 will show at once why the wind behind the cold front of a travelling depression is from the given quarter.

We have been describing the gust-lull structure of the northwesterly in the last sections and this theory enables us to understand many of Walker's observations, viz 'Thus what is involved is a predictable alternation of wind phases from two different directions, rather than an erratic scramble of variations from many directions.'

That is the way to look at the airstream that is full of gust cells – as two winds one of which replaces the other alternately. In fact any variable airstream, whether it is the normal northwesterly pattern or any other pattern, can be simplified into alternate phases during each of which the wind is from one side or the other of the mean wind direction. What other patterns it is possible to detect will be gone into later. For now we must concentrate on the

gust and veer – back and lull

pattern of shifts that characterise the cumulus-filled northwesterly.

Whenever we beat to windward, a wind feature, whatever it is, approaches along the apparent wind direction. It is perhaps easiest to see this if you use your imagination and ride in a gust cell at A in Fig. 30.1. You travel forward the distance AB in the same time as the craft at C travels CB. Thus relative to C the gust cell is not only moving forward, say at 15 knots, but also sideways at something like a quarter of that speed. Thus the 'apparent course' through the gust cells is along CA and the stronger the wind the more parallel to the mean wind direction does the apparent course become. We need to have this idea in order to understand how it is that although you are headed obliquely across the coming cells they cross you almost as if you were stationary. Thus in Fig. 30.2 one craft (X) meets a sharp gust at P and another at Q, but then slices through the less obvious shift situation at R. However, he is routed directly for the next gust front at S. Another craft (Y), similarly placed to the first, meets a gust front at A, a lesser one at B and another full one at C. So while (X) met lull-gust-lull-gust then an unpredictable shift pattern on the division between two cells and another lull-gust situation, (Y) met lull-gust then a less definite lull-gust and then a more definite lull-gust. For this reason covering your opponent in a variable airstream is often a waste of time.

Here we see how the beating craft meets the gusts and lulls which are sometimes very good examples of the theory we have given, interspersed with shift patterns that are less definite but which can be reacted to, providing not too much reliance is placed on the first stab of gust air that is felt.

The idea that there is a kind of mini-front between one cell and the following one also leads to the idea of 'gust tongues'. The recognition of gust

Figure 30.1 *Imagine being an imp riding a gust cell at A. The craft C will travel towards you along the apparent course CA*

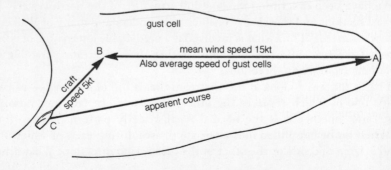

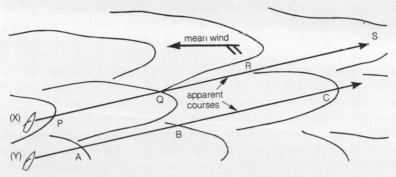

Figure 30.2 *How two craft (X) and (Y) beating through a sequence of gust cells meet different gust and lull patterns. This is why covering in variable airstreams is often a waste of time*

tongues is very important when beating to windward and tacking on heading shifts.

What happens is that before the gust proper arrives there is often a strong stab of gust air – the gust tongue – that has the tack-on-headers boats all crash-tacking from port to starboard as the veer that goes with the tongue heads them. However, often before they can complete their tacks the wind has gone back to what it was before or even further and in Fig. 29.2 there is a very good example of a gust-tongue event. For the gust and sudden veer at the two-minute mark is a gust tongue, and any port-tack boat who crash-tacked this sizeable header would be panic-tacking back again immediately as the wind went back further than before. From the anemogram we can see the true gust edge coming along at three minutes with its continuously veered wind favouring starboard tack for a relatively long time. Here the gust tongue arrived maybe forty seconds ahead of the true lasting shift.

In Fig. 30.3 we see another typical tongue event. There is a very definite lull before the tongue veers the wind at 45 seconds. Yet ten to fifteen seconds later the wind has gone back anticlockwise to such an extent that the boats that have just crash-tacked will be hopelessly headed. Yet had they used the tongue as a warning that a real gust front was in the offing they could have put up with a temporary bear-away as the tongue headed them and then more than made up for it as the wind backed immediately prior to the true gust front arriving. Now the wind stays up and stays veered, favouring starboard tack, for half a minute and then backs for twenty seconds before veering again and staying veered or close to the mean direction for a much longer period.

The thing we learn from thus analysing the real wind is:

When the wind shifts, wait twenty seconds or more before tacking.

This way you will gain more than you lose. If the puff is ephemeral, like a

169

gust tongue, you temporarily sail the wrong way, but do not run the risk of being put in irons if you attempt to tack. When the real shift comes along it will last for much longer than twenty seconds and you can take full advantage of it.

Gust tongues appear wherever the onward rushing gust air falls over itself and bursts through the gust front (G in Fig. 29.5). You can understand this if you imagine rushing forward and suddenly finding your feet in soft sand. As your lower extremities are held back, the upper body moves on and falls forwards towards the ground. In the gust's case it rolls over the top of the surface air that is held back by contact with objects on the earth. Very similar things happen on a grander scale with cold fronts. The cold air driving in under the warm air becomes held back by surface friction and sends big squally gusts out ahead of the line of the front proper. If you

Figure 30.3 *Another gust tongue event showing at (a) how a craft would respond to the shift pattern shown in (b). The letters refer to the phases of the shifts. Gust tongue D is a header. One craft tacks to this while the other hangs on and even though he bears away at E ends up at H with the true gust front to which he tacks. He also gets it first while the other craft meets it at H¹ and is well behind. X represents the distance the gust front moved from the moment H to the moment H¹*

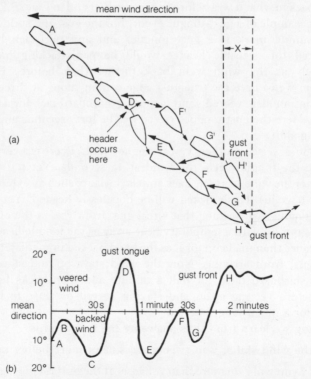

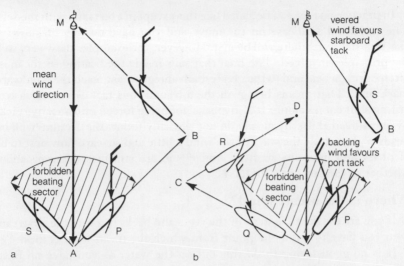

Figure 30.4 *(a) With a steady wind there is no advantage in sailing anything other than simple legs as you wish, but with a variable wind (b), board P adopts the correct tacks to meet the shifts and sails at some 30–40° to the mean wind rather than at 45° to it. Board Q does everything wrong and makes half the windward way that P did*

have a menacing line of cloud that looks like a cold front, allow for such squalls.

The correct tack to be on when the wind shifts clockwise (veers) is starboard and when the wind shifts anticlockwise (backs) to the other side of the mean wind direction it is port that is favoured and these reactions follow because they allow us to sail into the usually forbidden 'beating sector'. In Fig. 30.4a we assume that a steady wind blows from the windward mark M and that a craft at A can sail on either tack at 45° to this wind. If the wind is truly steady then sailing two legs AB and BC on either tack will take exactly the same time. There is no advantage in tacking other than once.

Now let us assume for the sake of argument that on the same course the wind is for the first half backed by some 15° to the mean wind direction. Now the craft on port tack can sail a course 15° inside the previously forbidden beating sector. Thus he sails PB and then the wind suddenly veers through 30° to come from 15° on the other side of the mean wind direction. Now starboard tack boats are sailing 15° inside the beating sector. If the previous beat in the steady wind took 10 minutes then this one in the variable wind takes only $8\frac{1}{2}$ minutes. Thus we see:

> In a backed wind port tack is favoured.
> In a veered wind starboard tack is favoured.

In practice no race can be sailed like this except in a test tank with models. The real wind is always on the move and you have no way of knowing exactly what shifts there will be in it. However, the examples show very well the principles involved. The boat that sails inside the beating sector most often during a beat and to the greatest advantage, must reach the windward mark first. That means being on the advantageous tack whenever a real lasting shift comes along. It also means not being forced into abortive tacks by short-lived shifts. It means do not slavishly follow the dictum 'tack on headers', but study the ways of the wind a little and so learn how best to be in phase and harmony with it. And if you are still in a dilemma about whether to tack or not – DON'T.

Where is the Mean Wind?

If you are to take advantage of the veers and backs in a variable airstream then you have to know the point from which the mean wind comes.

It is no good trying to do this out on the water as you have no fixed reference point. If the club has an anemometer or you can get sight of the dial of a masthead windvane on a yacht in a marina, you can watch the way the wind shifts backwards and forwards and find the average direction. Otherwise flags on club, craft or on the masthead of dinghies parked in the pound can give the required information. If the race is to be sailed within a mile or so of the point from which you make the observations then try to locate some landmark at long range that is in the eye of the mean wind.

With NW winds the visibility is good so a hilltop, an island, a large building etc. ten miles or more away, may stand out very well. If you do have a reference point as far away as ten miles then you can wander sideways by a mile and the angle from the true wind direction is only a matter of 5° which is less than the error in locating the mean wind direction anyway.

Only shifts that are 10–15° or more either side of the mean direction are going to be important to tack to, so to all intents and purposes your landmark will always be in the eye of the mean wind assuming of course that the direction does not change during the race. Most NW winds stay fairly constant in direction once they are established, but you ought to get a forecast of what the wind is expected to do over the time involved.

If your dinghy has a deck compass then the mean wind direction can be set on that which means you can wander wherever you like and still know whether the wind is veered or backed from the average direction. However, do not lose sight of the fact that the way to think of a variable airstream is as being composed of two winds (neither of which is the mean wind) that alternately replace one another. From this viewpoint the mean wind is going to be occasionally experienced. For almost half the time the wind will be veered and the other half it will be backed, spending little of the time around the direction that is half way between them.

31 Usual and Unusual Wind Patterns

The 'northwesterly' airstream in which the wind tends to veer when it gusts and to back when it lulls exhibits the behaviour we expect of the wind in the Northern Hemisphere. There is a very good reason why the wind should act this way, not only when the direction is from a quarter where convection currents are bound to form in it, but many other times as well.

The reason is tied up with the history of gradient and surface wind given in Chapter 29. The surface wind blows at an angle across the isobars out of high and into low whereas the gradient wind blows along the isobars. As gradient wind is assumed to be blowing in a deck from about 2000 feet upwards, while the surface wind is blowing in a shallow layer some 30 feet deep, the convection currents, that easily reach up to 2000 feet or more and induce corresponding sinking currents, can fetch chunks of gradient wind to the surface.

Air may be a fluid, but it has momentum and just like an arrow it flies on in the same horizontal direction and with the same speed as it descends. Thus in the Northern Hemisphere gusts will come from a direction that is veered to the surface air because the latter is blowing at perhaps 30° or more across the direction of the gradient wind in towards low pressure. Tactical reaction therefore is to expect a lift on starboard tack when the wind increases suddenly and to correspondingly expect to be headed and have to bear away or tack when on port.

The structure of gust cells indicates that while port tack is favoured as the wind lulls it is much more difficult to recognise the slower backing shifts that eventually result in the true lull. Here is where a distant indicator of where the mean wind is coming from is so useful – so that you have some idea when the wind has gone back past the mean direction. Even then you will need to ignore the turbulent eddies that will tend to mask the true direction of the shift.

What we have been describing is the normal, natural way the wind gusts and veers, backs and lulls so we will call this the normal wind pattern. It is the way most airstreams will act whether they are recognised as being full of gust cells or not.

When the wind grows and starts to blow hard it often clouds over at the same time. The cloud base is darkish and rather lumpy with skeins of scud underneath and the cloud is due to turbulent billows in the air produced by the high wind speed. The wind is always veering and backing in such airstreams, but there is no recognisable pattern that can be predicted. Each micro-shift comes along so rapidly that all you can do is to take advantage of those that favour you and do your best with the rest. Even if more permanent shifts occur there is no guarantee that the wind will swing back the other way in a short while. The shift may indeed by permanent as far as sailing the leg of a race is concerned.

There are similar indeterminate gust and lull patterns of relatively short duration when the upper clouds are gathering ahead of a coming front. I remember my mother forecasting the incidence of bad weather because the 'smoke is blowing down' and there is a definite tendency for sinking currents ahead of bad weather situations. Such currents must bring the gradient wind to the surface with an attendant veer, but again there is rarely any recognisable pattern. Bad weather sailing is from a micro-wind angle non-tactical. You just sail by the seat of your pants (or, on a board, by the soles of your shoes) and hope you can get more lifts than the others.

So having outlined some situations where the wind shifts are in no way susceptible to prediction, let us look at another airstream that is perhaps the most variable of all and which has a recognisable pattern about it. This is the easterly.

Now the 'easterly' is no more always blowing from the east than the 'northwesterly' is blowing from NW, but the way the wind shifts is typical of easterlies whatever actual direction it comes from. It has long been recognised by sailing people that when the wind goes east (which is against the normal westerly pattern that is natural for the world) it seems to go odd, but why should this be?

We may find part of the answer in the way the wind tends to have a shift pattern exactly opposite to the one described for the northwesterly. There the wind tended to veer as it gusted and to back as it lulled. We cannot usually talk about gusts in easterlies because the wind does not increase suddenly in the way we expect with a gust. Rather there is a slow increase lasting over several minutes with quite of lot of spikey increases and decreases as it hesitantly advances towards the new speed. The decreases in speed are equally slow and in between the wind will stay around the increased or the lulled speed.

The direction changes are linked to the speed changes in the exact opposite manner to the ones described for the northwesterly. For the easterly the rule is:

Increase and back – decrease and veer.

This is odd behaviour and sometimes the wind will go practically calm for several minutes before spiking up again to maybe something over 10 knots. Once you have this abnormally-behaved wind you will not forget it as it seems to get up to the oddest antics. However, the ideas given here should help to make the abnormal wind understandable from a tactical sailing point of view.

A typical abnormal easterly is shown in the anemogram Fig. 31.1 and we see that it is a very different pattern to the northwesterly. For one thing it is far more sluggish, with the wind wandering in a slow succession of shifts from one phase of the pattern to the next. It is far more like two different winds, one of which alternately replaces the other, than was the northwesterly even though it helps to think of the latter that way.

We cannot speak of gusts and lulls in this case because the wind increases are not at all like gusts in that they come about quite slowly in a series of swings towards the new speed and direction. Then the wind stays around the direction it has acquired for a minute or two before beginning to sink in speed and it may go almost calm for a while before beginning to pick up again.

Figure 31.1 *Comparison between the normal wind pattern of the northwesterly and the abnormally variable easterly*

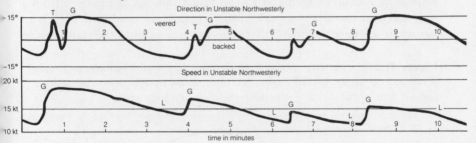

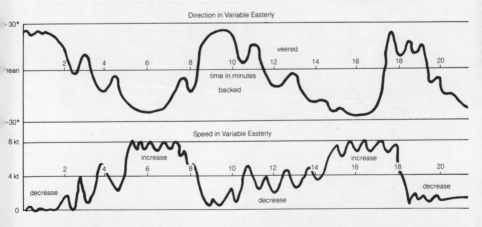

From a tactical viewpoint this is the airstream with the greatest potential for making gains (if you catch the shifts correctly) at the same time as it is the one where a mistake can cost you very dear. There may be 30–40° between the two phases of the shift pattern and the shifts come at a longer time interval than with the westerly pattern.

The 'easterly' is in some ways more difficult to recognise than the westerly and it rarely grows cumulus clouds. It is often very warm for the time of year and can be hazy. It shows its attributes most during the mornings when there is still an inversion layer holding down the surface airstream and I have found that on the South Coast of England it is often present before a seabreeze comes in against it. We can have 'easterly' characteristics with winds that are from NW to N as well as when the winds actually come from somewhere between SE and NE. Again we must be clear that the term 'easterly' denotes a type of airstream with attributes that can be recognised and which exhibits a certain predictable shift pattern.

The easterly is a truly tactical airstream because the winds are often light to moderate and so one is not tending to miss signs of shifts in the struggle to fight the worst excesses of a strong wind. Here you have to think it out and, with some knowledge of what is likely to happen, plan ahead somewhat.

Through analysis of the shifts shown in Fig. 31.2a, I have drawn the courses of two dinghies S and P who sailed through the pattern from a well-laid start line CD to a mark M some 1½ miles to windward. As it is an 'armchair' exercise the boat S that is on starboard tack at the start is given

Figure 31.2 *An easterly with shift phases that last some 8 minutes or so can, if you do everything right as craft S has done, make up a lead of 6 minutes in half an hour's beat. Craft P is assumed to do everything wrong*

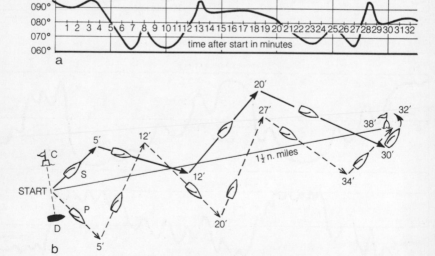

the benefit of always doing the right thing in the wind shifts that come along. The boat P that goes off on port tack starts wrong and against all the odds of luck always manages to do the wrong thing. Thus they end up at the windward mark with the bad luck boat almost six minutes astern of the paragon who could do no wrong.

Actual events would never see such a discrepancy because no one could be as good (or lucky) as S and no one (one hopes) could be as bad (or unlucky) as P. However, the exercise shows the absolute necessity of reading the wind shifts and taking the correct tack.

With the northwesterly there is a sudden wind increase to forewarn that the next few minutes should be ones with veered wind that make starboard the correct tack, but with the abnormally variable easterly there is no such warning. There are sudden increases in wind, but they herald the backed (port tack) phases rather than anything else. So you adopt the 'wait and see' policy first advanced for dealing with the northwesterly, but here it is even more appropriate. For after a veered phase where you have sailed on starboard tack as much as possible (ignoring the headers that forced you occasionally to bear away), there must be an almost equal backed phase with really big shifts backwards and forwards as it happens. So, as you expect this airstream to stay for some minutes (the one shown alternated every 8 minutes or so), you can afford to wait for as much as half a minute on what you know is an unadvantageous tack to make sure that it really is a true shift and not an ephemeral puff that will be back to what it was before in a few seconds.

For this reason, if no other, you cannot expect to sail a perfect tactical course in the variable easterly, but once you have recognised that you have this airstream you can expect to have shift phases that will follow very closely the idea that here are two winds that alternately replace one another.

32 The Performance Diagram and Tactics

If you already know something about sailing – and even if you do not – you can get much basic information about your craft and how to sail it on any point of sailing from its polar performance diagram. Because the latter shows the performance on all headings the relative speeds on any heading can be seen at a glance, and you do not have to go into great technical detail to appreciate the differences between one type of boat and another.

Luckily, unless you are a designer trying to wrest the last ounce of performance from a design (and there are very few such) you do not need to know the exact shape of the diagram for your boat. This is because there are only three basic shapes for the conventional craft we sail (Fig. 32.1):

a is the 'butterfly' of the planing dinghy and that for a board is very similar,
b is the 'circle' of the deep-keel yacht,
c is the 'lozenge' of the catamaran.

The butterfly comes about because of the enhanced speed V_s of the dinghy or board when the apparent wind is strongest and it planes with lowered skin friction (Fig. 32.2). So the distance travelled in unit time is greatest when the boat heading (γ) is between 60° and 90° to the true wind direction V_t. (The angle γ (gamma) and V_s and V_t are more or less standard symbols for these quantities.) When the dinghy is not planing, its performance diagram tends more towards the circle of the deep keel yacht which always sails with displacement performance.

The catamaran is a device that is almost always planing and its performance increases tremendously with even a slight reach off the wind so that the butterfly of the planing dinghy spreads sideways into the lozenge shape shown in Fig. 32.1c. As catamarans are rather special cases of planing dinghies we can ignore them for the moment and concentrate on the butterfly and the circle.

We can pick up a few more useful attributes of the performance diagram from Fig. 32.3. It is probably not absolutely correct in detail, but for most puposes detail is not important. It is the shape that is paramount.

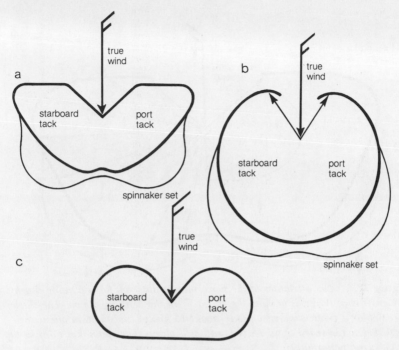

Figure 32.1 *The three basic shapes of performance diagram:*
(a) The butterfly shape of the planing dinghy (and the conventional board)
which becomes more complex when a spinnaker is hoisted.
(b) The lonzenge shape of the catamaran (shown without spinnaker).
(c) the displacement-sailing yacht which is almost equally good on all points
and to which only a spinnaker can make a difference.

You will see that when the wind speed is low (say 5 knots) the diagram is very close to a circle because the dinghy will not plane. If you have a high performance boat with a long waterline then even in low wind speeds this part of the diagram will bulge out more like the diagram does in stronger winds, because long boats and boards plane earlier and more easily in the lighter winds.

You can tell if such tactics are worth it if the performance diagram has any re-entrant regions such as A and B in Fig. 32.3. Let us assume you want to sail on heading OM. As the time to reach the envelope of the diagram from O (where you are supposed to be at time zero) is the same on any heading so it is an advantage to sail heading OR rather than OA and correct your overall course by occasionally heading OU. You go further in the same time on headings OR and OU than you do on OA. So 'tacking' across wind has advantages, but they are in reality not as great as you might think because the wind in which boats are supposed to sail according to their performance diagrams is a steady one of the kind found in the wind tunnels of

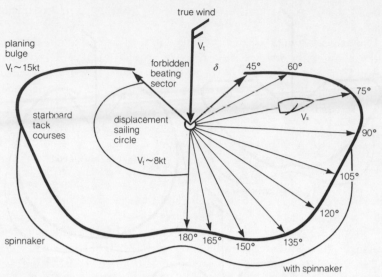

Figure 32.2 *The attributes of the performance diagram for a planing dinghy. The craft is at 0 and is making the speed V_s on the heading shown. The thick curve is for a given wind-speed (say about 15 knots) and the thin one is the shape below the speed at which the craft will plane. The spinnaker adds to the off-the-wind performance*

tank-testing laboratories. As the wind shifts its direction so the performance diagram also oscillates about O and we shall see that this has a profound effect on the basic ideas culled from performance diagrams.

Thus the performance diagram bulges in its very broad reaching sectors when a spinnaker is hoisted and tacking down wind then confers an advantage. The port tack side of Fig. 32.3 for the planing dinghy differs from the starboard tack side because the former is considered to be carrying a spinnaker whereas the latter is not. We see from these examples that boats that hoist spinnakers modify their performance diagrams and can make re-entrant zones so that the direct course on broad reaching and running headings may not be the fastest course.

Which brings us back to making way to windward. The diagrams sketched here have come from various books, but especially from C. A. Marchaj's book *Sailing Theory and Practice*. They were carefully researched and measured by the design boffins so we can believe in them. Wherever there is one of these re-entrant dents we can draw a line to touch the diagram as in Fig. 32.3. The 'forbidden' sector of directions 45° either side of the true wind is the biggest dent of all and we see at C in Fig. 32.3. that most way appears to be made in the direction of the true wind, when hard on the wind and possibly when within a few degrees off this direction. So hard-on-the-wind appears to be the way to sail the planing dinghy to windward. Even a slight reach gives no advantage in way made to windward.

The diagram should be mentally fixed to the wind direction and rotated as the wind shifts, but the only wind direction you have is given by the masthead flag or vane and is the apparent wind. A reasonably accurate assessment of the true wind direction can be obtained from the apparent wind using the following rules:

When beating – add 10° to the apparent wind direction
to find the true wind direction.
When close reaching – add 20° or less.
When broad reaching – add 30° or less.

These values do not vary tremendously with the range of conventional craft and they are near enough for most purposes.

With the performance diagram in mind you will, with a dinghy that sets a spinnaker, have two sectors of headings on either tack which will gain you way in those directions. These occur where the lines have been drawn in Fig. 32.3 across the re-entrant portions of the curve.

These sections will be named as in Fig. 32.3 so that we have a reaching sector which is about 10° wide and within which the maximum way is made when planing. Added to this is a spinnaker reaching sector which is some 15° wide and occurs around 110–120° to the true wind.

If making for a mark in the direction OM then more way is made by sailing on alternate reaching and spinnaker reaching courses even though you will be sailing a greater distance. However, there is a snag. The wind is

Figure 32.3 *The zones in which a craft's heading can wander and yet still make good way are here called reaching and running sectors. There is a normal reaching sector applicable to all boards and dinghies. There is a spinnaker reaching sector for those dinghies that carry spinnakers and there are running sectors as shown. Tacking across the wind pays with a spinnaker, but not without one, and tacking downwind pays with or without a spinnaker*

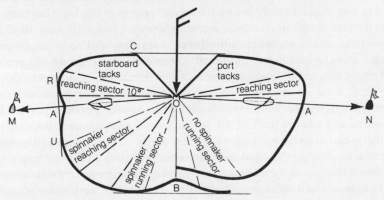

always shifting backwards and forwards and this will rotate the diagram between the two sectors even if you sail dead for the mark M.

For example, if the wind gusts and veers the diagram rotates, so that sailing OM you will automatically be sailing close to if not actually in the reaching sector when on port tack. You will get the best plane and the best course simply by making no alteration of course. As the wind backs, the diagram backs with it and so the boat sailing towards M will eventually get into the spinnaker reaching sector. Thus on port tack when broad reaching across the true wind little alteration of course is required, but good spinnaker drill is essential plus the ability not to be panicked into dousing the spinnaker by an ephemeral gust tongue.

On starboard tack things are different. Now when the wind veers the diagram rotates clockwise while the craft stays heading towards mark N and the spinnaker reach becomes favoured. This means that in the height of the bluster you are going to be setting a spinnaker with all that entails. So starboard tack is less favoured in a gusty airstream for this technique – just because of the practical difficulties involved. However, the well-drilled crew will gain here substantially. Now as the wind eases and backs (the diagram rotates anticlockwise) the reaching sector approaches the course OM and you will again be making as much as you can in the circumstances.

Of course with a short dinghy which will not plane in lowish wind speeds the boat may only sail displacement in the lulls even though it planes in the gusts. This will rub out the advantages of being in the reaching sector and there will be no advantage gained from these tactics as there will be no re-entrant region.

Obviously in practice the heading may be anywhere across the wind, but the principle expressed above will help sort out what changes of course may be advantageous and which may not.

The other re-entrant portion of the curve appears when sailing down wind. We have port and starboard running sectors that are some 20° wide and if you stay within that quite large angle of 20° you will make the maximum practical way you can. Whether a spinnaker is set or not there will be less way made directly before the wind because of the fact that the sails trap pockets of still air and there is less airflow over them. Bearing off either side of the dead-run course introduces more flow and so greater way is made. Thus tacking down-wind is advantageous providing you stay around 20° either side of the dead-run course. That means being 20° either side of the true wind all the time. Again the wind will shift backwards and forwards. When the wind veers (usually the heavier periods) port tack is favoured and when it backs it will pay to gybe onto starboard. Because you visualise the diagram rotating with these shifts you may not need to make much alteration to the dead-run course as the wind shifts will move you from one to other of the advantageous headings compared to the true wind.

The days when most people afloat in small boats were in two-handed dinghies with foresails and often with spinnakers are over. There is a great trend towards single-sail dinghies and by definition a board is a single-sail craft. Except for experiments one cannot see boards carrying spinnakers although they might fly further if they did. Thus the most likely shape for your craft is the simple butterfly. This immediately does away with the spinnaker reaching sector. There is then one and one only fastest sector of headings when reaching. The advantage in tacking downwind also becomes less as the re-entrant portion there diminishes in depth when a spinnaker is not set.

So what does the theory of wind shifts tell us about making most way across the wind when the fastest headings lie in the simple reaching sector? We see at once by mentally rotating the diagram clockwise with a veering shift that to make maximum cross-wind way you have to alter course with it making the necessary adjustment to heading to keep yourself in the reaching sector or as near to it as practicable.

This means on port tack bearing away as the wind veers assuming that you are already within the reaching sector and correspondingly making up as the backing phases come along. On starboard exactly the opposite is indicated so that you make up in the veers and bear away in the backing phases.

Making Way to Windward in a Variable Wind

'Thus when on a tack sailing towards an expected heading shift a boat should be sailed free and to leeward of the fleet'.

So says Stuart Walker in the book we cited at the beginning of this chapter and such advice might come as a surprise to many who are accustomed to beat to windward as hard on the wind as they dare. How can we make more way to windward by bearing away from the close-hauled course?

The operative words here are 'towards an expected heading shift' because such a technique only works when the wind is a true 'northwester' with a real recurrent shift pattern that more-or-less alternates between two directions as outlined in Chapter 31.

To show what Walker meant look at Fig. 32.4. A craft at A experiences a veering shift and instead of making up into it he holds his course to B thus making the amount AF towards the windward mark M. The veering shift freed him on starboard tack and so he sails free and to leeward of boats that are holding the hard-on-the-wind course AD. As the wind has veered so he expects it to back at the next major shift which occurs at B. Having waited a little and decided that it really is the major shift he expects he comes about onto port tack and again frees off so making the amount FM to windward. The boats that flogged along the beating course ADE end up well down on the one which took the more flamboyant, but well-reasoned course of freeing off and letting the wind do the adjustment of the courses for him.

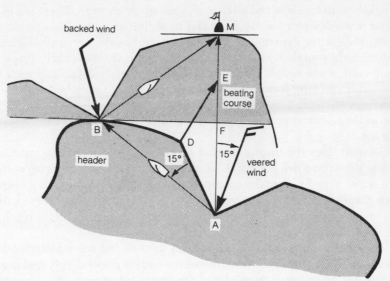

Figure 32.4 *Why the technique of sailing free and to leeward of the fleet works in a variable airstream*

Obviously it depends on being on the correct initial tack which is why on a variable day it is important to establish at the start where the true mean wind is blowing from. However, all is not lost because if you tack on prudent headers then whatever initial tack you are on, sometime soon you must tack on a header that gets you onto the correct tack. The problem then is to wait for and recognise the true shifts. The technique is perhaps even more important when the wind is lighter, but very variable as in the 'easterly' (Chapter 31).

33 Variable Winds in the Southern Hemisphere

Some of the changes to be expected in the antics of variable winds when you sail in the Southern Hemisphere have already been mentioned in passing, but in this section we give the modifications under one head.

As with the Northern Hemisphere it is mainly the temperate latitudes where the theory of variable winds apply. These are also the latitudes where a good deal of Southern Hemisphere sailing is done so what we are saying will be applicable to a large number of sailors south of the Equator.

Lows and highs exist and drift eastwards round the hemisphere, but the winds at the surface rotate round them in the opposite sense to the Northern Hemisphere. As in Fig. 33.1a the winds at the surface spiral out of high into low pressure centres while those at around 2000 feet follow the isobars. This latter is the gradient wind and is the one which is brought down by convection cells as gusts. The terms 'veer' and 'back' are used in exactly the same sense in the Southern Hemisphere as they are in the Northern and so as in Fig. 33.1(b) the gradient wind is backed to the surface wind – the exact opposite of what happens in the Northern Hemisphere.

Thus in the Southern Hemisphere the normal wind's variations are:

Gust and back – veer and lull.

Hence the higher speed phases tend to favour port tack while the slower ones favour starboard tack. This certainly indicates that international helmsmen who go to take part in races in the opposite hemisphere to the one in which they habitually sail will have to unlearn a good deal of what, for them, has become instinctive reaction to the wind's normal variations. Whether one recognises that there is generally a lift on starboard tack when the wind increases in the Northern Hemisphere or not, the experienced helmsman or board sailor has drawn this into his instinctive reactions. Because there is 'a luff in a puff', so a heading shift that is not too far ahead may not necessarily force a boat to bear away under its impetus. On

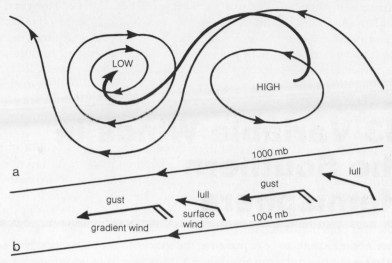

a

b

Figure 33.1 *(a) The way winds spiral out of highs into lows in the Southern Hemisphere.*
(b) How the gust and lull pattern is opposite to the Northern Hemisphere

starboard tack a puff that is backed (as it is more likely to be in the Southern Hemisphere than in the Northern) need not force one to bear away very much if at all. A backed shift where the wind drops in speed, however, is far more likely to force you to bear away substantially to meet it. As these effects are on opposite hands in the hemispheres so the wind's normal variable pattern will feel odd to one brought up exclusively in the other hemisphere.

Equally, of course, the long-period shifts that come when fronts and troughs pass are opposite to those in the other hemisphere:

> Winds veer as fronts pass in the Northern Hemisphere.
> Winds back as fronts pass in the Southern Hemisphere.

So when you recognise that the wind shift under an imminent cold frontal edge is about to occur then port tack is best in the Southern Hemisphere whereas it is starboard in the Northern Hemisphere. These tacks will obviate the risk of suddenly being put in irons by the coming wind shift that is driving forwards under the leading edge of the cold front. Similar remarks apply to warm fronts and occlusions, but often with these the shift is not so marked nor so sudden.

Just as in the Northern Hemisphere, a backing wind and a falling barometer go before the big blow because the wind in the previous ridge of high pressure will be from some easterly point and will back northerly as the low pressure troughs come in from the west. The air masses of Australia are something like those of say Europe, but they get different names. In Fig. 33.2 a typical summer chart shows tropical maritime (Tm) air and the attributes of this are like maritime Tropical air in Europe. However, in southern Australia because of the long land fetch of such winds, the Tm air becomes much dryer and so is dubbed modified tropical maritime (mTm) air. The airmass equivalent to maritime Polar air in Europe is Southern maritime (Sm) air and is often cold and unstable so that we see a cold front between the two latter kinds of air mass. Other air masses that come from the centre of Australia will be hot and dry and just as in Europe are called tropical Continental, but other air masses that skirt the desert interior of the sub-Continent become modified as well by losing moisture.

Thus the weather of the Southern Hemisphere is very like that of the Northern with all the same features of lows and highs, troughs and ridges, warm and cold fronts etc. However, there are important differences in detail and as with any sailing venue that is unfamiliar it pays to find out as much as possible about the local variations when you intend to sail an exotic new area remembering that the smaller weather features will in some ways be the same as those you are used to while in other ways they will be different.

These differences may be 'global' due to being in the other hemisphere or they may be large-scale local effects caused by the special conditions of the area. One well-known one is the 'Southerly Burster' or 'Buster' of the New South Wales coast which occurs when a long trough of low pressure extends northwards across most of the continent. There is warm northerly air ahead

Figure 33.2 *Weather features and air masses of Australia on a summer's day*

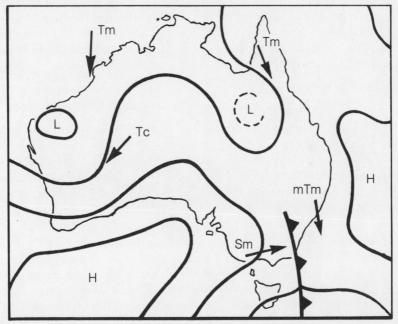

and cool southerly air behind this trough-line, but the danger of the Burster is that after a day or so of hot sultry weather and following the passage of the axis of the trough, the cool southerly comes up suddenly. It rises to strong to gale and the temperature may drop by some 20°F (10°C). It is also a phenomenon of the sailing season, that is, spring and summer, and while it may reveal its presence by a characteristic bank of cumulus cloud, it does not have to do so. Such local effects are due to large-scale pressure systems crossing an area, but there will be much more localised effects caused by special topographical features or the proximity of cool or warm ocean currents near a coast etc.

These cannot be gone into in detail here and so we will not mention them further but anyone who sails a coast, a river, a lake or reservoir etc. with which he is not familiar can make a great deal of sense out of local effects if he studies a map and uses the ideas of wind flow, stable and unstable conditions etc. and applies them to the chosen scene. Even then there will be minor trends that only the locals know about, but which will make the difference between being a winner or a loser. You may have to buy a pint or two in the clubhouse to discover what they are.

34 Waves and Wave Tactics

Waves are generated by the wind and within reason the stronger the wind the higher the waves. However, it is not only height of waves that is important. In fact for short craft like boards and dinghies it is steepness of a wave's profile that will make for the biggest problems.

Waves become important when they:

 i impede windward way,
 ii need to be met correctly for tactical advantage,
 iii contribute significantly to duckings or capsizes.

The waves that exist are the result of two factors:

a sea – which is generated by the wind that exists, plus
b swell – which is due either to a recent blow or is being fed in under the sea waves from some distant point.

Larger waves than average and smaller ones than average are due to the superposition of sea and swell (Fig. 34.1). Swell (a) is often longer in wavelength than sea (b) so when they are added we have to add their heights or amplitudes and the result is something like (c) which is dubbed 'seaway'.

Sea rises and falls with the wind so that when, as happens, a virtual calm descends after a gale, only swell is left and this also dies with time.

In small waters, because the distance the wind has to build waves (the fetch) is restricted, sea is not usually a problem and swell only enters via harbour entrances and estuaries. Even then the loss of energy by shallowing and deflection from the shores means it dies away very rapidly as the distance increases away from the open sea.

Where sea is a problem for dinghies and boards is when a creek lies in the direction of the wind and the tide runs strongly against the wind. Then a wind-against-tide seaway develops.

On the open sea waves are usually so long in wavelength as not to constitute a danger, but the short, steep seas generated by wind-against-tide conditions are often difficult to meet. However, even in restricted waters a

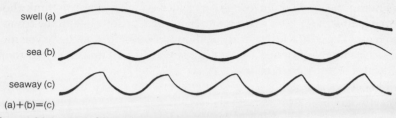

Figure 34.1 *By adding the sea to the swell we arrive at the seaway which is the real wave field*

perfectly reasonable wave system in a west-going channel with say a SW wind can turn very nasty if it curves to face the full fetch of the SW blow and the tide is running against it at a couple of knots or so (Fig. 34.2).

Sailing off the beach onto the open sea can induce similar effects when a coastwise tidal set builds up against the wind. A forenoon race with the tide flooding with the wind makes for very easy wave conditions, but the tide turns say over lunch-time and the afternoon – with perhaps no more wind – sees capsize after capsize amongst the dinghies in tumbling white waves.

Wave Tactics

The waves that have to be met are sometimes important in that those who take account of them and sail through them as efficiently as possible will make way over those who do not. Using the impetus of the wave that comes up on the quarter to initiate a plane that otherwise would not have been possible or which would have come a little later is an example of the use of waves to help save the seconds. When driving to windward the slap of a steep-fronted wave on the weather bow can effectively slow a dinghy, and the smaller the craft the more likely this will be.

There are however more subtle considerations. When sailing to windward the useful mnemonic is:

BC – AD

This means that the wind comes more from the Beam on the Crests and more from Ahead in the Depths of the troughs.

Figure 34.2 *How the wind-against-tide effect shortens and steepens the seaway*

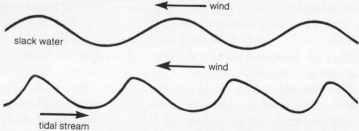

Thus at the crests of longish waves, where you have time to think about reacting effectively, you can hope to point up a little, while in the troughs you have to bear off a little. As these alterations of course also help you meet the waves more efficiently, so taking a slightly undulating course through the wavefield is good tactics.

This effect also applies to reaching as well and once the crest has run beneath, you bear away to make up on the steepening side of the next wave. When running, the shifting of crew weight becomes important as well so that the crew will throw their weight forward as the bow lifts and will then quickly move their weight aft as the wave passes and you surge down its leading edge.

Much of this depends on the time between one wave crest and the next and there is a well-known relation between the period (T seconds) of the waves and their length (L metres)

$$L = 1.56 \, T^2$$

This means that the wavelength has to increase very markedly to double the time between waves so that a wavelength equal to the length of a Flying Dutchman or similar big dinghy would find the waves passing any stationary point every 2 seconds. However, when the period is twice that the waves have lengthened to 25 metres (80 feet) and doubling the time period again to 8 seconds increases the corresponding wavelength to some 100 metres (100 yards).

The shorter the wavelengths the more difficult they are to meet and when going to windward the length is effectively shortened by the boat's speed to windward. When we combine the known attributes of waves and the boat speed over the ground to windward we can deduce the time period between succeeding crests (or troughs) from a simple set of graphs (Fig. 34.3).

These cover wavelengths from 25 metres (80 feet) to 100 metres (330 feet), but as no small-craft helmsman can independently assess wavelength while he is sailing, only the two things he can know, namely his own forward speed and the time between crests, are important. We see from Fig. 34.3 that the waves have to be long to provide a reasonable time between one wave and the next. We also see that at 6 knots waves over 100 metres or yards in length pass every 6 or 7 seconds. That is half the time it takes to tack so you cannot hope to tack in any part of a single wavelength. Further, the technique of slightly altering course, making up a little on the crests and bearing away a little in the troughs, is an advanced one and it will come well down the beginner's list of priorities.

Turning back now to wind against tide. If a tidal stream sets you at 2 knots into the wind then effectively you must add 1½ knots to what you think your forward speed is to find the time of meeting the waves. So if you think you make 6 knots, then you enter the graphs at 7½ knots and find it makes a difference of about half a second. In other words being set against the waves

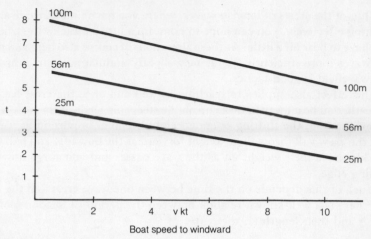

Figure 34.3 *Graphs to find the time (t) between wave crests when beating to windward at speed (v) kt for waves which are either 25, 56 or 100 metres (yards) from crest to crest*

and wind at a couple of knots is not going to shorten the time of meeting the waves very much. This is because waves travel so fast and only very short waves (which means very frequent waves) will travel at anything comparable to dinghy speeds even planing before the wind.

While the time period *is* shortened due to the wind-against-tide phenomenon, it is the effect on the waves themselves that is most important. Waves are a visual sign of wind energy and the grip that the wind has on the water depends on their relative speeds. Push the water against the wind and the wavelength must shorten, but the energy involved between wind and water increases somewhat. This increase in energy appears as heightened waves of shorter period. Stand on the shore of a creek where the tide is setting out strongly against the wind and you see what happens to the wave field. It becomes full of white horses that are not evident in anything like the same numbers elsewhere. The wavelength and frequency of waves when the wind is against the stream anywhere (and this is particularly dangerous off headlands and promontories where there are tide races or in restricted 'funnels' where the water has to flow through narrows), make for a difficult passage as the distance between one crest and the next is often not much more than the length of the dinghy or board. When conditions are near to the extreme for the class of boat involved it is here that many capsizes occur and the strength of the tidal stream makes for potentially dangerous situations. This is just another instance where you must stay with the craft and not try to make shore – good advice under almost all circumstances when you capsize.

Index